WRITING RESUMES THAT WORK

A How-To-Do-It Manual for Librarians

Robert R. Newlen

***HOW-TO-DO-IT MANUALS
FOR LIBRARIANS***

NUMBER 82

NEAL-SCHUMAN PUBLISHERS, INC.
New York, London

Published by Neal-Schuman Publishers, Inc.
100 Varick Street
New York, NY 10013

Printed and bound in the United States of America.

Library of Congress Cataloging-in-Publication Data

Newlen, Robert R.
  Writing resumes that work : a how-to-do-it manual for librarians /
by Robert R. Newlen.
        p.   cm.—(How-to-do-it manuals for librarians ; no. 82)
  Includes index.
  ISBN 1–55570–263–5
  1. Library science—Vocational guidance—United States.
2. Résumés (Employment)—United States. I. Title. II. Series:
How-to-do-it manuals for libraries ; no. 82.
Z682.2.U5N49   1998
650.14'024'092—dc21   97–51220
                                                              CIP

CONTENTS

LIST OF FIGURES

To my parents:
William M. Newlen (1919–1998) and
Betty M. Newlen (1922–1995)

FOREWORD

Robert Newlen has written the most important and valuable resource for anyone seeking employment in libraries today. *Writing Resumes that Work: A How-To-Do-It Manual for Librarians* is all that any job seeker will need to be successful. The first four chapters offer detailed and practical tips on resume preparation through the use of worksheets designed to guide the reader in the creation of a document which is certain to capture the attention of the prospective employer. Chapters five through ten, however, are likely to be the most useful to some. Each addresses a particular category, e.g., library school student, non-supervisory librarian, special librarian, etc., and offers sample resumes as well as specific guidelines.

The most critical stage in the employment process for the job seeker, especially one who is new to the profession, is the one in which the employer reviews resumes to select the small number of candidates to be invited to be interviewed. To be successful at this stage requires that one have a resume which demonstrates that the applicant is one among this small number worthy of further consideration. Often well-qualified applicants are passed over in this stage because their resumes do not convey their qualifications and special abilities for the position. This manual offers both a process for preparing a resume which will assure qualified candidates come to the attention of prospective employers and a number of practical guidelines for helping each individual reader to apply the process to his or her particular situation.

Newlen brings considerable experience in three areas to the writing of this manual: as a manager who has hired a number of staff, as a counselor and mentor to job seekers, and as a designer and presenter of workshops on writing resumes. It is obvious that his experience as a trainer in this area is what makes this book such a valuable tool. The reader is guided through a series of exercises, for which worksheets are provided, to create the best possible resume. Newlen believes that an effective resume is a marketing tool and that as such it must be tailored for each position and prospective employer. His process for creating the document is designed to make it easy for the job seeker to make the necessary adjustments to prepare a special version for any position vacancy.

This book will help librarians create resumes which will lead to interviews. It will also benefit managers and administrators who review so many resumes. I anticipate that it will upgrade significantly the quality of resumes in the profession. This manual is essential for every librarian.

Maureen Sullivan
Organizational Development Consultant

PREFACE

Writing Resumes That Work: A How-To-Do-It Manual for Librarians is designed to simplify the process of resume writing for librarians and information professionals; its ultimate goal is to help the reader create a resume that will land that all important job interview. Through easy-to-follow steps, the resume writer learns from this book how to build a job-winning resume tailored to a job objective and to the needs of a potential employer. The emphasis is on creating a flexible resume, one that can be easily customized to meet changing needs. It is intended for librarians at all stages of their careers, from library school student to library director. And it covers all areas of librarianship—public, academic, school, special, and all others. An optional disk provides templates of the resumes presented in this book that can be customized to meet individual needs.

The book is organized as a series of exercises. The first one is for the resume writer to compile personal data and define the job objective. The next consideration is the substance of their resume, and it includes defining skills needed to meet the job objective and identifying personal accomplishments that support those skills. Next comes an examination of various resume formats along with guidelines to assist the resume writer in choosing the one that best showcases individual talents and qualifications. Finally, results of all the exercises are assembled to create the final product. A wide range of sample resumes are given, all of them based on those of "real life" librarians. Tips for writing resume cover letters are also considered.

This process for writing resumes is based on my experience in giving resume-writing workshops for librarians, counseling individual librarians on how to write resumes, and as a library manager who hires employees. Competing in today's job market is no easy task, and I hope librarians will find that this book makes the process less stressful.

ACKNOWLEDGMENTS

This book began over a strawberry daiquiri at the Fountainebleau Hotel's pool in Miami Beach. Thanks to Pat Schuman for buying me that drink and taking me up on this project. No one could ever ask for a more encouraging editor than Charles Harmon, and I am grateful for his guidance and patience. Thanks to all of those kind friends and colleagues, particularly those in the District of Columbia Library Association, who shared their resumes so I could have "real life" examples. I am grateful to colleagues from the American Library Association and those on the Staff Development Committee of the Personnel Administration Section, Library Administration and Management Association, especially Charles Beard, Mary Frances Burns, Melissa Carr, Joan Kaplowitz, Erlene Bishop Killeen, Susan Wardzala, and Jim Walther. I also appreciate the support of my family and friends as well as colleagues at the Library of Congress and the Congressional Research Service, particularly Lea Barber, Vanessa Cieslak, Pamela Dragovich, Angela Evans, Judith Farley, Jeanne Hamilton, Lynne Kennedy, Lynne McCay, Barbara Morland, Dan Mulhollan, Betsy Reifsnyder, Jill Roberts, Kent Ronhovde, Donna Scheeder, Michelle Springer, Brenda Wesner, and Kristen Whitney. And to Nancy Davenport, who encouraged me to explore uncharted waters, my deepest gratitude.

INTRODUCTION

Heights.
Flying.
Death.
Insects.

These are four among the ten things humans in the United States most fear, according to David Wallechinsky in *The Book of Lists*. I was quite surprised to discover that resume writing was not included. Based on my experience conducting workshops on this topic for librarians, I can't think of anything that strikes more fear in the heart of the prospective job seeker than resume writing. But perhaps this should not come as a surprise, since the resume—if done correctly—can be an effective marketing tool that will help land an interview.

Even though resumes are often the first introduction to employers, I'm constantly amazed at how casually some job seekers treat them. I've seen resumes printed on paper that was a perfect match for my Uncle Maury's pink Cadillac; resumes with grease stains (were they chowing down on chips while writing?), typos, and grammatical errors; resumes that rivaled *War and Peace* in length—you name it! Remember: a potential employer may have only twenty seconds to review a resume, so make it concise and appealing; treat that resume with the same reverence as Mom and apple pie.

So where to turn for advice on writing the job-winning resume? You don't have to look far—a whole industry has developed to exploit resume writer anxiety. The shelves of your local bookstore and library are overflowing with how-to guides that practically guarantee you a job with a starting salary of $50,000 minimum. And check out the dozens of resume services listed in the employment section of most major newspapers—experts who claim (for a small fee and your first born) they can design resumes that will have employers on their hands and knees begging you to take their jobs.

What makes this book different from all the others crowding the shelves? First, most tomes on this topic assume that one formula will work for everyone; I call these the "quick fix" resume books. They fail to recognize that every individual, as well as prospective employer, is different, and that resume writing is not one-size-fits-all. Your experience, education, accomplishments, skills, and job objectives are unique. But how do you create a resume that is tailored to your unique needs—and those of your prospective employer? *Writing Resumes That Work: A How-To-Do-It*

Manual for Librarians will guide you step-by-step through a series of exercises that will provide the building blocks to create a customized resume. But resume substance won't be our only concern. We will also carefully examine the *look* of the resume: Is it visually appealing? Does it jump out at your prospective employer?

Another feature distinguishes this book. Most standard resume guides attempt to cover every job category imaginable in one book, and if they include librarians and information professionals at all they're usually relegated to the "other" section. This book is written specifically for librarians. The dozens of sample resumes you will review are those of real librarians (with names and places changed to protect the innocent!) and are drawn from the full spectrum of library positions, at all career stages, and from a wide range of areas—academic, public, school, special, law, and the like. While your final resume may not resemble any of these examples exactly, it can use them as models. The accompanying disk of sample resume formats will help you tailor your own resume. No matter where you are in your career—library school student or library director—*Writing Resumes That Work* can work for you.

While resume writing is not an easy process, you probably already have all the tools you need to start writing now. Forget the "professional" resume writer—most employers who routinely review resumes can spot these products a mile away. And you don't need costly computer programs to create the job-winning resume—all of the resumes in this book were completed using WordPerfect on my home computer. Be prepared for some hard work, though, and tough decisions. And remember that the resume is *you*. Do you want that first impression to be a typo or misspelled word? In this competitive job market, settle for nothing less than the best. Now, let's get to work!

1 GETTING STARTED: THE FIRST STEP TO A JOB-WINNING RESUME

In this chapter we will:

- define the resume
- review the exercises you will complete to build the resume
- compile a personal inventory.

First, let's define the purpose of the resume and how it can be used most effectively. When is it appropriate and not appropriate to use the resume? How does your knowledge about the potential employer influence how you write the resume? Next, we will outline a series of nine step-by-step exercises, the results of which will provide you with the elements necessary to create the job-winning resume. Then you will complete the first of these exercises: taking a personal inventory of your life. This inventory is critical because it serves as the foundation for the subsequent exercises, and you will be referring back to it constantly. It could be the most time-consuming exercise, but well worth the effort.

WHAT IS A RESUME?

Webster's defines the resume as "a short account of one's career and qualifications." To put it even more succinctly, the resume is YOU. Since the primary purpose of this document is to land an interview, every decision made about the design or content of the resume should be made from *the employer's perspective*. Put yourself in the employer's shoes: How can you show that you are the most qualified? What have you achieved that makes you the greatest asset to the library? How will you benefit the organization? Does your resume set you apart from the dozens of other resumes scattered about the employer's desk?

Many job seekers think that one generic resume can be used for a variety of positions and employers, that one resume can suffice if you're only applying for similar positions in one type of library. Wrong! Why not? Because each library, each employer is different; this means that each resume you write must be custom tailored to address each one's special needs. Just listing your past job responsibilities and duties won't set you apart and show that you are the strongest candidate. And resume doesn't mean an account of your life history. Again, start thinking like the employer! Define your skills and abilities to demonstrate that you alone are the best qualified. Creating a custom resume for every position may seen daunting, but this book can help you streamline this process.

THE MULTIPURPOSE TOOL

Job applicants utilize resumes in many different ways. Let's review some of these uses, and the pros and cons associated with each.

The Blind Resume

The odds of landing a job by sending an unsolicited resume to an employer for an unknown position are roughly the same as winning the lottery. You probably will have more luck handing them to strangers on the street (and save on postage, too). Some job seekers succumb to the law of averages strategy: if I send out enough resumes, surely they will catch the eye of someone, somewhere, and I will get an interview. But "papering" as many employers as possible with a resume is the least effective use of the resume. One individual I know mailed over 200 resumes and never received a single response.

The major problem with blind distribution of resumes is that you're unable to identify a specific opening, therefore your resume becomes too generic. In addition, in this method it is virtually impossible to customize for the employer; the person reviewing your resume has to figure out how you might fit into their organization. Since that reader will probably spend less then twenty seconds with your resume, it is doubtful that he or she will exert this effort.

Resumes for a Specific Opening

A job seeker typically learns about a position in three ways: from an advertisement in a newspaper or professional journal, from a vacancy announcement in an organization employment office, or through other people. Knowing as much as possible about the specific opening and the library makes it much easier to customize your resume. Don't settle for what's described in the advertisement or vacancy announcement. Do a database search or take advantage of any contacts you have (networking!) to find out as much as possible. To start thinking like the employer, here are some questions to ask about the target library or organization:

The job-winning resume should . . .
- Set you apart from the competition
- Be an effective marketing tool to sell you
- Concisely present an overview of your accomplishments
- Focus on landing you an interview
- Be written from the employer's perspective
- Tell the employer why you are most qualified
- Be written in your own words

The resume should *not* be . . .
- An autobiography
- A listing of your job responsibilities or duties
- An account of every accomplishment
- An exercise in creativity
- A job description
- Your life history

- What are the overall goals of the library?
- How does the position contribute to meeting those goals?
- How does the library relate to its larger organizational entity (university, county government, etc.) or community?
- Who are the primary clients?
- What can you learn about the library from press accounts?
- What are the problems or challenges facing the library?
- What are the library's greatest successes?

Taking the time to learn as much as possible about the library will give you the information to give your resume the edge it needs to get the employer's attention. This information will also be useful in writing the cover letter, which we will discuss later.

Resumes for Interviews

Many job seekers find it useful to take a resume to the interview. In some cases, the employer will not have seen it before the interview. Faced with the need to quickly fill a position, I have often called applicants for an interview before I've seen their resume. In this situation, I review education, qualifications, and experience by referring to the resume, so it serves as a guide for the interview.

Some employers feel that the most effective use of a resume is sending it *after* the interview. Not only does this provide an opportunity for you to review and re-emphasize your qualifications with the employer, but also you are able to further customize the resume after learning more about the position and the library in the interview. This strategy has merit in some circumstances, but generally I don't recommend it. Most employers want a resume at the interview stage so they can compare it to those of other applicants. By the time the resume is received after the interview, the employer may have already decided on another candidate.

The "On Demand" Resume

Like the blind resume, the "on demand" resume precludes customization. Nevertheless, it's wise to have this type available for unexpected situations. For example, always have copies available at conferences or professional meetings. Take advantage of unplanned situations where your resume might come in handy—never miss an opportunity to market yourself! And never underestimate the fact that employers share resumes with other employers. Those who recruit or hire routinely are among the best networked group I know. An employer may be impressed with your resume but decide that you aren't the best qualified candidate for their particular position. However, if they become aware of other openings for which you might be qualified, they will typically pass your resume on to those employers.

STEP-BY-STEP EXERCISES TO BUILD THE RESUME

Let's define the specific steps you must take to create the job-winning resume. Follow each of these exercises in order—there are no shortcuts! They will give you the flexibility to try a variety of resume formats. Although this will be a time-consuming process initially, most of these steps won't have to be repeated each time you create a customized resume. This up-front investment will serve you well later.

STEP 1: YOUR PERSONAL INVENTORY

This exercise inventories your life and career. You will list all pertinent details related to your job history, education, volunteer and professional activities, publications, and so on.

STEP 2: DEFINE YOUR JOB OBJECTIVE

What is your specific objective and what role does it play in the resume? Should you always identify an objective on your resume? How will the employer interpret this information—can it be used to your disadvantage? We will answer each of these questions and assess how you should use the job objective statement.

STEP 3: DEFINE THE SKILLS OR QUALITIES NEEDED TO MEET YOUR JOB OBJECTIVE

Once you have defined an objective, what are the qualities that are most important for achieving it? You will identify the top skills needed and evaluate each one using knowledge of the employer.

STEP 4: IDENTIFY ACCOMPLISHMENTS AND ABILITIES THAT SUPPORT EACH SKILL OR QUALITY

To complete this step, you will review your personal inventory and write supporting statements about each skill. We will look at action verbs and techniques for succinctly communicating your strongest abilities.

STEP 5: WRITE THE SUMMARY OR HIGHLIGHTS OF QUALIFICATIONS

In this exercise, you will identify the top four or five qualifications that demonstrate why you are the best candidate for the job.

STEP 6: CHOOSE THE BEST RESUME FORMAT

Which resume format works best for you *and* for your potential employer? We will examine three different formats: chronological, a listing of your positions in reverse chronological order; functional, which highlights skill or quality categories; and combination, which contains elements of the first two formats. The strengths and weaknesses of each format will be evaluated vis-à-vis your career and resume needs.

STEP 7: ASSEMBLE THE RESUME

This is where we pull all the elements together and actually write the resume. We'll look at suggested headings for each category and decide what and how much information should be included.

STEP 8: HOW THE RESUME LOOKS

Once the content of the resume is complete, we'll evaluate its "look" to make sure it is visually appealing and attractive. We will also consider length, formats, tips on using graphics, and how to select the appropriate paper.

STEP 9: A FINAL CHECKLIST

After all the exercises are completed, we'll give it a final review to make sure it's in perfect shape.

Now, let's work on the first exercise!

STEP 1: YOUR PERSONAL INVENTORY

Before actually writing the resume, start by taking a personal inventory of your life. Don't panic! I promise you won't have to analyze your relationship with your mother. This inventory serves two important purposes. First, it's an excellent source to refer back to as you tailor your resume to specific job objectives and employers. Second, by reviewing the inventory before an interview, you can refresh your memory about your skills and accomplishments. You are going to look at each of the following areas in detail—a worksheet with each of these categories is included at the end of this chapter:

- professional work history
- nonprofessional work history

- education, specialized training, and language skills
- professional association involvement
- publications
- presentations
- research and grant activities
- volunteer work and personal interests

Obviously, all of this information won't be included, but it's important to get an overall picture so that you have all the building blocks ready with which to construct the perfect resume. If your job objective changes or you need to update the resume, this inventory will save you the trouble of reinventing the wheel. Bear in mind that certain personal information is not appropriate to include in your resume (see Appendix I).

Now, let's look at what should be included under each personal history category.

PROFESSIONAL WORK HISTORY

In reverse chronological order, list *all* position titles and organizations for which you have worked. Include dates of employment—generally it is sufficient to just include the years in the position (e.g., 1986 to present) and omit the specific months. Review your entire career; not all of these positions will necessarily appear on your resume, but we don't want to leave anything unexamined. Include a description of your accomplishments in this position. An easy way to do this is with "bullet" one-line descriptions. Your one-liners should be in your own words and *not* be lifted from a job announcement or be a laundry list of your duties. Consider the following questions in describing each of your positions:

- What are your responsibilities?
- How many employees have you supervised?
- Can you quantify your accomplishments? For example, how many people have you supervised? If you administer a budget, what is the amount? If circulation improved, by how much and over what period of time?
- What personal skills have you developed, such as working independently or on a team? Have you worked under pressure and deadlines?
- Did you initiate or implement a program or procedure?
- What leadership skills have you acquired? Have you chaired a committee or headed a special project?
- What have you accomplished outside of your required responsibilities or job description?

- List any special details or temporary promotions. Have you served in an "acting" position?
- Have you won any awards? This is not the time for modesty!
- What problems have you solved? How did you find solutions?
- Have you used writing skills?
- Have you done any public speaking?
- What are your automation skills? What types of systems do you have the most experience with?

Remember to account for periods of unemployment. Resume writers often neglect to mention periods of unemployment due to child care, full-time academic pursuits, and the like, but any significant gap in employment is a red flag for the potential employer, who will assume the worst—incarceration, undercover spy, or political terrorist, at the very least. While it is not necessary to indicate why you left a position in a resume, *always* be truthful if this issue is raised in an interview situation. This information can be verified and should be dealt with directly.

Finally, don't forget to include any consulting or freelance work. Have you done private research? Indexed a book? Prepared bibliographies for publications? These are all important skills, and you don't want to omit them from your resume.

NONPROFESSIONAL WORK HISTORY

Why mention that job delivering pizzas? Some job candidates shoot themselves in the foot by not revealing what they consider to be nonprofessional work experience because they fear they won't be taken seriously. True, including nonprofessional work experience on a resume is not appropriate for everyone, but for some job seekers (such as those just out of library school), these jobs can be part of your marketing strategy.

Positions such as waiter/waitress, receptionist, telephone solicitor, or camp counselor may actually have some relevance to the job you are seeking. Take the waiter/waitress position, for example. It requires juggling multiple demands and interacting with a wide range of people; can you think of better preparation for coping with the demands of the reference desk?

For a position involving extensive telephone reference, I once interviewed a candidate who mentioned in passing that she had worked as a telephone reservation clerk with a major motel chain. This information was omitted from her resume, but what better experience for telephone reference—I hired her on the spot!

EDUCATION, SPECIALIZED TRAINING, AND LANGUAGE SKILLS

List all degrees, schools, and dates of enrollment.

List any awards, scholarships, fellowships, internships, honorary societies, or superior grade point average. Did you participate in drama or debate?

List significant training courses, dates of completion, and skills acquired. Be sure to include a list of all database, software, and network training and your degree of proficiency in each. When it comes time to write the resume, remember to include only those courses that are directly relevant to the position you are seeking. Remember that automation classes are especially important. List language abilities and skills levels in each language, such as whether you can read or converse fluently. Indicate if you have lived in a foreign country.

PROFESSIONAL ASSOCIATION INVOLVEMENT

Frequently overlooked by job applicants, this is one area that can set you apart from the competition. Many resume writers list memberships in professional organizations yet neglect to indicate their level of involvement. A prospective employer is interested in learning about your level of participation in these associations because it demonstrates initiative and commitment to the profession.

Just like other types of volunteer work, you may have gained valuable experience through professional association involvement that has direct relevance to the position you seek. No opportunity to chair a meeting in your previous job? Then don't forget to mention that you chaired a committee in the Special Library Association, in a library school student association, or local library association. Your prospective job requires budgetary experience and you have no related duties in your current position? Then describe your position as treasurer of a regional library association. Don't forget that documenting participation in a professional association can make an instant connection with a prospective employer who is active in the same organization or who may have held the same position in another organization and thus understands the complexity and responsibility involved.

PUBLICATIONS

List the names and titles of any articles or books you have written. Be sure to include any experience in writing for association or staff newsletters. Keep a master file of these publications so you can quickly make copies when writing samples are required for applications or interviews.

PRESENTATIONS

List any presentations you have given at professional conferences, workshops, or seminars. Be sure to indicate the dates of these presentations. Also, include any courses you have taught or tours you have led.

RESEARCH AND GRANT ACTIVITIES

List any ongoing research. Have you received grants to support your research? Don't forget to mention these items. They are especially important for those applying for academic positions.

VOLUNTEER WORK AND PERSONAL INTERESTS

Like professional organization involvement, experience gained on your own time is often neglected by resume writers. Just because you weren't paid doesn't mean this experience isn't worthwhile. Documenting volunteer work is important for several reasons. Today, many employers look for well-rounded individuals, people with a healthy balance of work, school, and play in their lives—the direct opposite of the workaholic so revered in the eighties. Volunteer work also reveals valuable skills and leadership experience that is transferable to a paying job:

- organizational skills
- public speaking
- fund raising
- budgeting
- publicity
- meeting deadlines
- coordinating meetings
- planning for events
- leading a team
- recruitment
- training
- scheduling

Can you think of other skills you have gained in religious, charitable, or community groups? If you can successfully manage a group of children as Room Mother/Father in an elementary school, you can probably handle the many pressures of library work! Be sure to note how long you have been involved in these activities. To describe volunteer work positions, use the same process as described for professional positions.

List personal interests and sports activities. Again, including these may not always be appropriate (skydiving, bungee jumping, sword swallowing, and nude modeling are probably best omitted), but they can often make an important connection with a potential employer.

CASE STUDY: JANET TAYLOR

To illustrate how a personal history worksheet is developed, we will use Janet Taylor as an example here and in subsequent exercises so that you can follow the complete development of a resume step-by-step.

Janet is an assistant director of a medium-sized public library district, and she is seeking a position as director in a similar library system. She has the education, skills, and qualifications necessary for this type of position and is now faced with the challenge of marketing her strengths in the resume. Let's take a look at the resume Janet wrote before she completed the nine step exercises in this manual (see Figure 1.1).

Now imagine that you are an employer hiring for a public library director position. If you had plenty of time to carefully dissect it, her resume might reveal some of the qualities needed for her target position. But remember, the average resume reader will spend less than *20 seconds* with Janet's resume, so her qualifications must virtually jump off the page and grab the reader's attention. Briefly, here are some of the major weaknesses of this resume:

- Janet does not give a job objective.
- There is no summary of qualifications to demonstrate why she is the best choice for this position.
- The overall format is visually unappealing. The dates of her employment have too much emphasis.
- There are typos.
- Acronyms appear that may have no meaning to the prospective employer.
- Janet's accomplishments under each job read more like job descriptions.
- She has not elaborated on the extent of her involvement in the professional associations listed.
- She has included inappropriate personal information.
- She hasn't quantified her accomplishments.

Now, let's follow Janet step-by-step as she completes her personal history worksheet. As you will see, Janet omitted a great

---

Figure 1.1 Janet Taylor's "Before" Resume:

```
           Resume of
           Janet F. Taylor
           27 Chelsea Court
           Woodland Springs, AR 72764
           501-555-2828

                       Relevant Experience

Jan., 1991-        Assistant Director, Redford County Public Library
                   District

                   Serves on the newly created Library Building Com-
                   mittee.
                   Worked extensivly on implementing plans/services
                   for this new building. Created the Library's Di-
                   saster Plan, ADA Strategic Plan, In-Charge Manual,
                   and Supervisor Management Documents. Aides De-
                   partment Heads in creating job descriptions and
                   solving personal problems. Worked with the Main-
                   tenance Dept. to make their transition to the new
                   building easier.

1990               Acting Director, Redford County Public Library
                   District

                   (Jan.-June 1990) Negotiated the new building plans
                   through the political obstacles of Redford County
                   Public Library District. Submitted the first bud-
                   get ever that was passed on the first try by the
                   Trustees. Learned to balance Staff, Trustee, and
                   Community needs.

Feb., 1989-        Associate Librarian/Head of Technical Services
Jan., 1991         (Redford County Public Library District)

                   Worked actively on the new building referendum
                   with Staff, Trustees, and community groups. Learned
                   to manage a multi-faceted department.

1987-1989          Associate Librarian/Head of Reference
                   (Redford County Public Library District)

                   Worked with my Department to form a service-ori-
                   ented team and a more in-depth collection. Was
                   responsible for the Library's building renovation
                   in 1988.
```

<u>Other Experience</u>

Reference Librarian (1984-1987), and Elementary School Librarian (1982-1984). A variety of part-time positions between 1979 and 1982 include Substitute Refrence Librarian at Springdale College, Documents Technician at University of Arkansas Undergraduate Library.

<u>Education</u>

1975-1979   Grinnell College, Grinnell, IA (B.A.)
                Major: Sociology   Minor: Italian
                Member: Nominations Committee
                         Student Council
                         Choral Choir

1980-1982   University of North Texas School of Library Science (M.S.)
                Member: Library School Student Assoc.

<u>Membership and Committees</u>

American Library Association
Arkansas Library Association
   Staff Development Comm.

1992   "First Line Supervisors: On the Edge", LAMA Journal, Fall, 1992.

<u>Other</u>

Good health. Divorced with two children.

deal of significant information that will be useful in demonstrating that she is very qualified for a director's position. At this stage, she remembers that this is not the time to be selective. Her goal is to get everything down and edit later.

JANET TAYLOR'S PERSONAL HISTORY WORKSHEET

PROFESSIONAL WORK HISTORY

Janet has listed her complete work history and used bulleted one-line statements to describe her positions (see Figure 1.2). She is most concerned about inventorying—she can refine the descriptions of her accomplishments in later exercises.

NONPROFESSIONAL WORK HISTORY

This includes work experience not directly related to her field.

Admissions Office Clerk, Grinnell College, 1975–1976
- *Processed applications—entered tracking information in computer system*
- *Responded to telephone and letter inquiries from prospective students*

EDUCATION, SPECIALIZED TRAINING, AND LANGUAGE SKILLS

B.A., 1979, Grinnell College, Grinnell, IA. Major in psychology. Minor in French.

Debate team member, 1977–78
Member, Student Association Nominations Committee
Member, Oratory Choir

M.S. in Library Science, 1982, University of North Texas School of Library Science, Denton, TX.

Programs Committee, Library Science Student Association. Served on team that coordinated quarterly programs for students.

Figure 1.2. Janet Taylor's Worksheet (Professional Work History)

Assistant Director, Redford County Public Library District, Redford, AR
1991 to present

- Assisted Director in managing a budget of $4.5 million, a staff of 105, and a collection of over 275,000 items
- Worked closely with Board consisting of 7 members
- Library Building Committee—chaired this committee for 2 years
- Coordinated transition team to plan move to new building
- Designed Library's Disaster Plan
- Designed and implemented ADA Strategic Plan
- Wrote Supervisory Manual for the library
- Advised 5 department heads on writing job descriptions
- Counseled department heads on employee problems

Acting Director, Redford County Public Library District
1990

- For six-month period, served as Acting Director
- Negotiated the new building plans with Board and County government; worked closely with community groups on all aspects of building plan
- Proposed budget that was passed on the first vote by Library Board
- Responsible for all administrative functions of the library

Associate Librarian/Head of Technical Services, Redford County Public Library District
1989–1991

- Managed all aspects of Technical Service Department including acquisitions, serials, interlibrary loan, and cataloging functions
- Extensive use of OCLC and the Dynix automated library system
- Experience with AACR2 and MARC formats
- Extensive audiovisual cataloging
- Supervised a staff of 7
- Outstanding performance evaluation

Head of Reference, Redford County Public Library District
1987–1989

- Supervised a staff of 8 reference librarians and 4 library aides
- Served on the Collection Development Committee
- Chaired committee on user access
- Revised and improved library reference guide
- Developed and monitored database budget of over $25,000

Reference Librarian, San Angelo Free Public Library, San Angelo, TX
1984–1987

- Provided extensive reference service
- Coordinated staff training on new online catalog
- Redesigned quick reference collection for more efficient use

Elementary School Librarian, Sam Houston Elementary School, Eagle Pass, TX
1982–1984

- Developed and maintained library and multimedia center for school of 350 students
- Created Parent Advisory Committee for library to increase parent volunteers
- Implemented automated circulation control for the library

Substitute Reference Assistant, Springdale College, Springdale, TX
1981–1982

- Performed part-time reference services for college library serving 800 students
- Staffed reference and circulation desks
- Routinely used college automated catalog to assist patrons

Documents Technician (part-time), Grinnell College Undergraduate Library, Grinnell, IA
1977–1979

- Worked with Federal Depository Library collection
- Sorted and shelved documents
- Maintained collection

PROFESSIONAL ASSOCIATION INVOLVEMENT

While Janet's current resume reflects the breadth of her professional involvement, it doesn't reflect the extent of her activity.

American Library Association, 1987 to present

Member, Supervisory Skills Committee, Personnel Administration Section, Library Administration and Management Association, 1991 to present. Served on subcommittee that implemented a listserv on supervisory skills. Helped to plan and implement 1992 program at Annual Conference—"First Line Supervisors: On the Edge."

Arkansas Library Association, 1985 to present

Secretary, 1989–90. Took minutes of all meetings. Member, 50th Anniversary Committee. Served on team that planned and implemented Association events for celebration. This included a Tribute Day event involving Arkansas legislators and media.

PUBLICATIONS

Co-edited article on program presented at Annual Conference, American Library Association, "First Line Supervisors: On the Edge," Library Administration and Management Journal, *Fall, 1992.*

VOLUNTEER WORK AND PERSONAL INTERESTS.

Served for 2 years as volunteer for Reading is Fun program tutoring elementary school students on weekends (1989–90).

Through St. Mary Parish, coordinated volunteer visits to 3 nursing and long-term care facilities in Redford, AR (1992).

Personal interests: Embroidery, roller blading, travel, French language group

This is quite an inventory! You can see that when Janet started to analyze her background, she recalled a great deal of information that will be useful in her revised resume. This is the primary purpose of the inventory—to get the big picture so that you can pick and choose what is most relevant to your targeted position and employer. Now it's your turn! Use the following pages (Figure 1.3) to create your own personal inventory or create one on your personal computer or in a notebook. The personal history is hard work, but it will pay off when you move on to the next steps to develop resume content. Again, you will be referring back to this inventory throughout the building process. When you finally land that interview, your personal inventory will be an excellent document to review. So let's make the most of this inventory.

Figure 1.3. Step 1: Personal History Worksheets

PROFESSIONAL WORK HISTORY
- ✓ Include all positions even if you don't think they will be included in your final resume.
- ✓ "Bullet" your accomplishments and write them in your own words.
- ✓ Remember to account for periods of unemployment.
- ✓ Don't forget consulting or freelance work.

NONPROFESSIONAL WORK HISTORY
- ✓ This is especially important for library school students and those beginning their careers.
- ✓ Think about skills such as communication and organization that transfer to your target position.

EDUCATION, SPECIALIZED TRAINING, AND LANGUAGE SKILLS
- ✓ Include awards, scholarships, fellowships, and internships.
- ✓ Pay particular attention to courses related to automation.

PROFESSIONAL ASSOCIATION INVOLVEMENT
- ✓ Describe your level of involvement and any skills you have acquired.
- ✓ Remember to include any leadership positions you have held.

PUBLICATIONS, PRESENTATIONS, RESEARCH AND GRANT ACTIVITIES
- ✓ Be sure to include any writing you have done for association and staff newsletters and publications.
- ✓ For academic positions, don't forget ongoing research and any grant activities.

VOLUNTEER WORK AND PERSONAL INTERESTS

✓ Remember that skills you have acquired in volunteer activities are transferable to paying positions.

✓ List personal and sport activities—remember that these can make instant connections with employers.

2 THE RIGHT STUFF: RESUME CONTENT IN FOUR STEPS

In this chapter we will:

- identify your job objective
- define the skills and qualities needed to meet your job objective
- identify accomplishments and abilities that support each skill or quality
- write the summary or highlights of your qualifications

As we review each of these areas in exercises, we'll continue to use Janet Taylor as an example. Your personal worksheet for each of these exercises is included at the end of this chapter.

STEP 2: DEFINE YOUR JOB OBJECTIVE

This exercise is especially important because it will help you tailor your resume to show the potential employer that you have the necessary skills and abilities for the job. Your job objective should be stated in clear and succinct terms. The litmus test for anything that you include in the resume will be whether it supports that job objective.

The job objective statement can take two different forms. The first is fairly straightforward when you are applying for a specific position and you know the job title. Examples of these types of job objectives include:

- Library Director for Villanova University
- Technical Services/Automation Coordinator at the University of Pittsburgh
- Coordinator of Children's Services with Knoxville Public Library
- Assistant Professor of Library Science at the Catholic University of America
- Library Systems Administrator with the Prince Edward County Public Library

Specifically including the job title as your objective at the top of the resume shows the potential employer that you have taken the time to customize your resume to that particular position. This is an eye-catching strategy that makes a positive impression on the reader.

Writing the second type of job objective is more challenging and is used when you are applying for a particular type of position with several employers. This is tricky, because you don't want an employer to eliminate you from consideration for other positions because the job objective statement is defined too narrowly. Here are some examples of this second type of job objective:

- Automation librarian in a college or university
- Public services librarian with a specialization in bibliographic instruction
- Archivist/special collections librarian
- Entry-level reference position in a public library
- Bibliographer specializing in history and political science
- Document-delivery librarian in an academic library
- Collection development librarian
- Coordinator of reference services, with emphasis on business administration
- Cataloging position specializing in use of OCLC and NOTIS
- Library systems administrator specializing in UNIX-based systems
- Corporate librarian
- Children's librarian position with specialization in storytelling in public or school library
- Head of Technical Services in a public library system
- School library media specialist

So how do you define your job objective? Start by answering these questions:

- What do you want to do next?
- What type of library or organization do you want to do it in?
- At what level do you want to do it? Entry level? Supervisory or managerial level?

The important thing to remember is that the job objective should be *brief, clear, and to the point*—not generic. Some job objective statements to avoid include:

- A challenging position as a librarian that takes advantage of my education
- Position as an entry-level cataloger with career-enhancing opportunities
- Library management position that will utilize my people-oriented skills
- Position as young adult librarian with a rapid promotion ladder
- Entry-level reference position with outstanding training opportunities

Most of these statements reveal the applicant's expectations, not the employer's. Now let's take a look at Janet Taylor's job objective statement, which is fairly straightforward. Here are her answers to the questions listed above:

- What do you want to do next?

  Work in a position with greater supervisory and administrative responsibility.

- What type of library or organization do you want to do it in?

  A small or medium-sized public library.

- At what level?

  As a director.

With these questions answered, Janet's statement reads as follows:

Objective: Position as a director in a small or medium-sized public library.

STEP 3: DEFINE THE SKILLS AND QUALITIES NEEDED TO MEET YOUR JOB OBJECTIVE

Now that you've defined your job objective, it's time to determine the types of skills and qualities needed to meet it. Put on your analytical thinking cap, because this is one of the hardest parts of building the resume. Whether you are addressing a specific job opening or a broader job objective, this is the time to *start thinking like a potential employer*. What skills are the most desirable? You can determine this by observing what critical skills are identified in the job announcement. Think about the following:

1. Carefully review every aspect of your target position. What are the skills needed to be most successful in this position? Think of as many as possible and write them down.
2. Now, start prioritizing. Try and narrow your list down to four or five of the most important qualities or skills.

Let's look at some job objectives and the most important skills or qualities needed to be successful in that position (remember, concentrate on what the employer considers most beneficial):

Job Objective: Acquisitions department head in an academic library

1. Financial and accounting skills
2. Automated acquisitions experience
3. Supervisory experience
4. Coordinating acquisition procedures

Job Objective: Reference librarian specializing in health sciences

1. Reference skills
2. Background in health sciences
3. Oral communications skills
4. Searching skills with health-related databases

Job Objective: State librarian of Vermont

1. Budgetary experience
2. Managing a complex operation
3. Background in state libraries
4. Knowledge of automated systems and networked environments
5. Experience in governmental relations

Job Objective: Coordinator of instructional services and programs

1. Experience in design and implementation of instructional programs
2. Knowledge of technologies in teaching and learning
3. Background in networked and electronic environments

4. Supervisory skills
5. Knowledge of adult learning theories and instructional strategies
6. Writing skills

Job Objective: Internet librarian in a public or academic library

1. Training experience
2. Advanced Internet searching skills
3. Oral and written communication skills
4. Knowledge of networking and telecommunications issues

Job Objective: Head of children's services in a public library system

1. Ability to plan and direct children's/young adult collections
2. Supervisory experience
3. Knowledge of children's/young adult resources
4. Oral communications skills

JANET TAYLOR'S SKILLS AND QUALITIES

First, Janet does some brainstorming on the critical skills and qualities needed for this position:

Experience in a public library system
Fiscal management skills
Supervisory experience
Oral and communications skills
Ability to interact with community, library boards, and local governments
Leadership skills
Experience with automation
Organizational skills
Strategic planning

She then narrows the list to the following:

Supervisory and administrative skills
Community and government relations experience
Automation planning skills
Fiscal management skills

STEP 4: IDENTIFY ACCOMPLISHMENTS AND ABILITIES THAT SUPPORT EACH SKILL OR QUALITY

Having identified the most important skills and qualities needed to meet your job objective, it's now time to write supporting statements for each one. In other words, prove that you have the experience to do the job! Start by reviewing your personal inventory—your hard work on this earlier exercise is now going to pay off.

For each skill or quality, you are going to write several one-line supporting statements. Carefully analyze the experience you have acquired that is directly relevant to each one. Here are some essential tips for writing these one-liners:

1. Keep the language tight and phrases short.
2. Don't use the first person "I."
3. Use incomplete sentences like:

   > planned and implemented the network
   > initiated after-school reading hour
   > coordinated acquisition policies
   > evaluated network proposals
   > established cataloging policies
   > wrote bibliographic instruction training manual
   > administered budget of over $30 million
   > simplified archival acquisition procedures

4. Use action verbs such as: achieved, administered, compiled, converted, effected, expanded, improved, increased, planned, reorganized, streamlined, and trained. A comprehensive list of action verbs is included in Appendix II.

5. Avoid terms found in job descriptions such as:

   > Responsible for . . .
   > In charge of . . .
   > Duties included . . .
   > Scope of responsibilities included . . .

6. Use plain English and avoid "insider" terminology and acronyms that may have no meaning to the resume reader. Remember that the potential employer may not be a librarian and may have only limited or no knowledge of the field. Be specific and don't use vague phrases like:

Facilitated inservice computerized circulation

Represented the library on District Steering Team for the WPL–WASB Pilot Project

Established IMC routines

Determined community needs and services

Represented the section on interlibrary teams

7. Think about writing these one-liners in terms of your accomplishments. This is what will sell you to the prospective employer. Whenever possible, *quantify* your skills and illustrate your results. Demonstrate to your potential employer that you are action and result oriented:

How many people did you supervise?

How much money did you save?

What size budget did you manage?

How much did circulation improve?

How did productivity increase?

What did you produce?

How many students did you train?

What were the results of programs you implemented?

How much time did you save?

Instead of:	Use:
"Significantly boosted circulation in my library"	"Increased circulation by 20,000 titles in two years."
"Looked at library automation systems and hardware"	"Evaluated and recommended an automated circulation system that was selected."
"Created bibliographies on several subjects"	"Wrote bibliographies on current national defense and foreign affairs topics on a continuing basis."
"Supported the technical services section"	"Participated on team that accessioned new materials and prepared materials for cataloging."
"Changed procedures for checking-in serials"	"Successfully streamlined procedures for serial check-in which saved 8 hours of staff time a week."

8. When you have worked with a team—say so! If you coauthored a report, be sure to indicate it.

9. Don't be modest. However, be wary of using too many superlatives; while you may be "the most productive" or "the most innovative," it's better to demonstrate how and why you are productive or innovative.

10. Don't exaggerate or, worse, lie. Never include anything you wouldn't want printed on the front page of the *New York Times*.

JANET TAYLOR IDENTIFIES HER ACCOMPLISHMENTS AND ABILITIES

To achieve her goal of a position as director of a public library, Janet identified the following skills and qualities:

Supervisory and administrative skills
Community and government relations experience
Automation skills
Fiscal management skills

Using her personal inventory, the following are one-liners that Janet wrote for each:

Supervisory and administrative skills
- *Wrote comprehensive library disaster plan*
- *Assisted in administration of a staff of over 100*
- *Coordinated transition team to move central library to a new building*
- *Chaired library building committee and submitted plan that was approved by library board*
- *Wrote supervisory manual for the library*
- *Counseled department heads on employee problems*

Automation skills
- *Evaluated library automation systems and made recommendation that was accepted*
- *Helped to implement installation of Dynix automated system*

Community and government relations
- *Designed and implemented ADA Strategic Plan*
- *Met monthly with library board*
- *Represented library on Redford County Business Development Committee*
- *Negotiated building plans*

Fiscal management skills
- *Assisted in managing a budget of $4.5 million*
- *Co-chaired audit review committee*
- *Proposed a budget (1994) that was passed on the first attempt by the library board*

STEP 5: WRITE THE SUMMARY OR HIGHLIGHTS OF QUALIFICATIONS

Not to be indelicate, but the summary of qualifications is where you grab the potential employer by the throat and say, don't pass over this resume, because I've got what it takes to do your job! The summary of qualifications is your opportunity to self-market. Since these highlights appear just below the job objective, this is one of the first resume elements that the reader will see. Once again, you need to think like the employer.

To help you write the qualifications, review Step 4 and match your most outstanding accomplishments—four or five statements are best—with the skills you perceive to be most important to the employer. This is no time to be modest! Be brief and to the point, and highlight your strongest qualifications as they relate to the job objective. If a statement does not specifically reinforce the job objective, eliminate it. Every qualification must be focused on your objective.

Here are some examples of job objectives with a summary of qualifications.

Job Objective: Reference librarian specializing in health sciences
Summary of qualifications:
- *Three years experience working in reference in major medical school library*
- *Expert searching experience with a wide range of health databases including OVID and NLM*
- *Developed innovative training and instructional manuals in print and electronic formats*
- *Strong educational background in health sciences*

Job Objective: Supervisory government documents librarian
Summary of qualifications:
- *In-depth experience in working with a federal depository collection*
- *Extensive background in cataloging government documents and maps*

- *Supervised a staff of 7*
- *Ability to work well in fast-paced, high pressure environment*

Job Objective: Interlibrary loan librarian
Summary of qualifications:
- *Strong skills in working with integrated library computer systems*
- *Excellent knowledge of copyright law*
- *Broad knowledge of document delivery systems and networks*
- *Two years experience in electronic document delivery*

Job Objective: Associate professor of library and information science
Summary of qualifications:
- *Graduate teaching experience at large university*
- *ABD in Library Science*
- *Extensive experience in information retrieval systems and services*
- *Well known for innovative teaching techniques*

Job Objective: Head of children's services in a public library system
Summary of qualifications:
- *In-depth knowledge of children's literature and services*
- *Five years experience as branch librarian with specialization in service to children/young adults*
- *Extensive supervisory experience*
- *Developed award-winning reading programs for children*

JANET TAYLOR'S HIGHLIGHTS

After carefully checking to see if each qualification supported the job objective, Janet chose the following:

Objective: Position as director in a small or medium-sized public library.
Summary of qualifications:
- *Outstanding supervisory and administrative skills gained in dynamic, medium-sized public library*
- *Extensive experience in evaluation and implementation of automated systems*
- *Assisted in managing a budget of over $4 million*
- *Proven skills in government and community relations*

Worksheets follow to assist you in completing Steps 2 to 5 (Figures 2.1 to 2.4). When you are finished, turn to the next chapter, on choosing a resume format.

Figure 2.1. Step 2: Your Job Objective Worksheet

✓   Keep it brief, clear, and to the point.
✓   Don't describe your career or job expectations.

**Figure 2.2. Step 3: Skills and Qualities Needed to Meet Your
Job Objective Worksheet**

✓   Think like potential employers—what are their expectations?

Figure 2.3. Step 4: Accomplishments and Abilities that Support Each Skill or Quality Worksheet

✓ Write several one-line supporting statements for each.
✓ Use incomplete sentences.
✓ Quantify your accomplishments whenever possible.
✓ Use action verbs; see Appendix II.

Figure 2.4. Step 5: Summary or Highlights of Qualifications Worksheet

✓   Write four or five statements that highlight your strongest qualifications as they relate to the job objective.
✓   Focus on your job objective

3 THE RESUME FORMAT THAT SELLS YOU

You are getting closer to bringing all the parts of the resume together, and it's now time to make some format choices that will market you best. Because selecting the best format is important, this chapter is devoted to helping you choose the best format. We will examine three different formats, learn how to integrate them with the results of the completed exercises, and weigh the pros and cons of each so you can choose the one that best fits your individual needs.

STEP 6: CHOOSE THE BEST RESUME FORMAT

You will choose one of the following formats:

- chronological
- functional
- combination

There is no agreement among experts about which format is best. The bottom line for choosing a resume format is which one sells you and demonstrates why you are the superior choice for the position. The format you choose should give you the flexibility to customize according to your specific job objectives and the needs of the employer. I know I'm starting to sound like a broken record, but remember to keep thinking like the potential employer. If you are having trouble deciding which format is best, try all three. Since you have all the building blocks, do a side-by-side comparison, and see which one is most effective. Remember, there is no right or wrong format—only the one that demonstrates that you are best for the job!

To illustrate each of the formats, we're going to leave Janet Taylor for a moment and look at the example of Daryl Jones. We will vary his job objective to demonstrate how each format can be customized to support that particular objective and highlight his most relevant experience.

CHRONOLOGICAL RESUME

The chronological resume is basically a listing of your jobs in reverse chronological order. It is the most popular resume format.

Pros:

1. The chronological format is easy to read and write. Many employers feel that is the most accessible format.
2. It calls attention to job progression. It is particularly useful to show job promotions and increased responsibility.
3. It can draw attention to the fact that you currently work for a prestigious library or organization.

Cons:

1. The chronological format may be least desirable for those who have been in one position or institution for a long time.
2. If there have been gaps in employment, this format can accentuate them.
3. It can make all of your jobs appear to have equal weight, i.e., it may emphasize a job that you really don't want to highlight.
4. It does not work well for those who are changing careers. If you are looking for a position in a different field of librarianship, it is generally not a good strategy to focus on your current position.
5. If your current job title is vague or doesn't adequately reflect what you actually do, the chronological format will accentuate this.
6. It doesn't always highlight your major skill areas.

Chronological Format Case Study: Daryl Jones

Daryl's job objective is to work as a project leader for a national program related to the digital preservation of state historical documents and images. He currently works in a prestigious institution, has had steady progression in his field of librarianship, and has some experience related directly to the position he seeks. He particularly wants to draw attention to his current position. Therefore, Daryl has chosen the chronological format (see Figure 3.1).

These are the two positions he feels are most relevant to his job objective. His earlier positions will be identified in summary form under a work history heading.

Figure 3.1. Sample Chronological Format

Senior Research Librarian, 1991–present
The Library of Congress, Legislative Reference Service

- Extensive reference service, including in-person assistance, to members of Congress and congressional staff.
- Specialized in issues related to arts and education.
- Expert searching skills using a wide range of databases such as NEXIS, WESTLAW, and Dialog. Use of Internet protocols and resources: Gopher, World Wide Web, and e-mail.
- Experience with archival and special format materials using Library of Congress and other collections related to film, photographs, and music.
- DOS, Windows, and Macintosh proficiency for research and technical support.
- Supervisory experience in delegating and reviewing work of librarians.

Special Assignment, Team Member, User-Evaluation Special Project, 1991–93
The Library of Congress American Image Project

- Evaluated American Image prototype (an electronic version of archival materials in Library of Congress collections).
- Chaired site selection subcommittee, prepared report, and presented results to senior managers.
- Coordinated orientation and training sessions at Library and at selected sites throughout the United States.
- Wrote sections of instruction manual, interviewed site coordinators, analyzed site experiences, and was one of three authors of final report.

FUNCTIONAL RESUME

The functional format is useful for highlighting skill or quality categories and draws attention to your accomplishments. Review Step 4 and choose the three or four major skill areas that best support the job objective. Include one-liners under each skill area to showcase relevant experience from any of your previous positions.

Pros:

1. This format is particularly useful if you have been in one position or one institution for a long time. It focuses on the range of skills and experiences you have acquired there.
2. Works well for the career changer, because it demonstrates transferable skills. This type of resume doesn't focus on the most current position, which may not be relevant to a new career goal.
3. For those re-entering the job market, this format can be particularly useful because it provides the opportunity to include volunteer experience in the skills descriptions.
4. It generally makes employment gaps less noticeable.
5. If you have switched jobs constantly or had a series of part-time or temporary positions, this format will not emphasize that fact.
6. This is one of the best formats for library school students or those with limited job experience.
7. It can de-emphasize a current job title that may be outdated or not adequately reflect your responsibilities.
8. If your jobs are unrelated and don't reveal a distinct career path, this may be the format for you.

Cons:

1. Some employers are suspicious of this format and think the resume writer may be hiding something (like a major gap in employment).
2. Some consider this format to be less accessible than the chronological format.

Functional Format Case Study: Daryl Jones

Daryl's job objective has now changed and he is focusing on a position that is somewhat of a shift from his traditional career path. His objective is to work as a film librarian at the Academy of Motion Picture Arts and Sciences. Although he has worked in a film library, the experience is not recent. Some of his recent experience has been with film research, although it has not been the primary focus of his position. For these reasons, Daryl has chosen the functional format (see Figure 3.2).

Figure 3.2. Sample Functional Format

Film Reference and Research

- Provided in-person and telephone reference service in major university film library.
- Created major bibliographies on film history, production, and personalities.
- Examined and prepared special collections inventory of Ritz Radio Theatre disk recordings.
- Excellent research skills with archival and special format material using Library of Congress and external collections related to film, photographs, and music.

Database and Internet Searching

- Extensive searching experience including use of NEXIS and Dialog.
- Use of Internet protocols and resources: Gopher, World Wide Web, and e-mail.
- DOS, Windows, and Macintosh proficiency for research and technical support.

THE COMBINATION RESUME

The combination format is just that; it combines elements of both the chronological and the functional. Like the chronological format, you lead off with your most current job and then indicate your skill areas as subheadings.

Pros:

1. Like the functional format, the combination can be useful if you have been in one position or institution for a long time.
2. Provides the advantage of highlighting distinct jobs as well as skill areas.

Cons:

1. This format requires special care in how it is presented graphically.

The Combination Format Case Study: Daryl Jones

Assuming once again that Daryl's job objective is to work as a project leader for a national program related to the digital preservation of state historical documents and images, let's see how the combination format looks (see Figure 3.3).

You can now see that one of these formats will give you plenty of flexibility to tailor your resume to a specific job objective.

Figure 3.3. Sample Combination Format

Senior Research Librarian, 1991–present
The Library of Congress, Legislative Reference Service

Reference and Research
- Extensive reference service, including in-person assistance to members of Congress and congressional staff.
- Specialization in issues related to arts and education.
- Experience with archival and special format materials using Library of Congress and other collections related to film, photographs, and music.

Automation
- Expert searching skills using a wide range of databases such as NEXIS and Dialog. Use of Internet protocols and resources: Gopher, World Wide Web, and e-mail.
- DOS, Windows, and Macintosh proficiency for research and technical support.

Special Assignment, Team Member, User-Evaluation Special Project, 1991–93
The Library of Congress American Image Project

Project Evaluation
- Evaluated American Memory prototype (an electronic version of archival materials in Library of Congress collections).
- Chaired site selection subcommittee and presented results to senior managers.
- Coordinated orientation and training sessions.

Writing
- Co-authored instruction manual for digital prototype.
- Wrote final report for the project.

JANET TAYLOR'S FORMAT

You will recall that Janet's job objective is director of a small or medium-sized public library. She has been with one institution for a long time, which might suggest that a functional resume would be best. She has held several progressively responsible positions within her library, however, and she wants to emphasize that fact. Janet has decided that a combination format would best meet her objective (see Figure 3.4); note how she has listed a main heading for her library that is not repeated with subsequent positions; this helps to emphasize her promotions in one institution.

Figure 3.4. Janet Taylor—Combination Format

Redford County Public Library District, Redford, AR

Assistant Director, 1991–present

Management
- Assisted in daily management and administration of over 100 staff.
- Coordinated transition team to move central library to a new building.
- Chaired library building committee, developed strategic plan, and presented plan to library board.
- Wrote comprehensive supervisory manual and library disaster plan.
- Served as Acting Director, 1990.

Automation
- Planned and implemented installation of Dynix automated system.
- Led team that evaluated library automation systems and made recommendation that was accepted.

Community and government relations
- Designed and implemented ADA Strategic Plan.
- Represented library on Redford County Business Development Committee.
- Negotiated building plans with community review board.

Fiscal management
- Assisted in managing a budget of $4.5 million.
- Co-chaired audit review committee.
- Proposed a budget (1994) that was passed on the first attempt by library board.

Associate Librarian/Head of Technical Services, 1989–91

Management
- Managed all aspects of technical service department including acquisitions, serials, interlibrary loan, and cataloging functions.
- Supervised 7 staff members.
- Outstanding performance evaluation.

Cataloging and Automation
- Extensive use of OCLC and the Dynix automated library system.
- Experience with AACR2 and MARC formats.
- Extensive audiovisual cataloging.

Head of Reference, 1987–89

- Supervised a staff of 8 reference librarians and 4 library aides.
- Served on the collection development committee.
- Chaired committee on user access.
- Revised and improved library reference guide.
- Developed and monitored database budget.

Janet decided that her jobs held prior to 1987 should be listed under an "Additional Work Experience" heading.

You've made remarkable progress! Having chosen your resume format, you're ready to pull all the pieces together and to write the first draft.

4 PUTTING IT ALL TOGETHER: THE FINAL STEPS

In this chapter we will coordinate the results of the exercises you have completed and actually write the resume. Then we'll look at tips to make sure your resume looks sharp and give it a final once-over before you give it to the potential employer. Finally, we'll talk about the sample resumes that follow this chapter.

STEP 7: ASSEMBLE THE RESUME

Don't relax yet! You've created most of the pieces, but now you must exercise great care in how you assemble them. In this section, we will look at the arrangement of the major headings of the resume. Following are some general guidelines to follow as we consider each part:

1. Remember the maxim of the great architect Mies van der Rohe: "Less is more." While it is important to support your job objective fully, resist the temptation to include every detail. Use concise, to-the-point language.
2. Use plain English—avoid flowery language, arcane professional jargon, and acronyms that aren't universally recognized.
3. Each heading should be bolded and you may want to consider using all capital letters (see resume samples).
4. Separate each heading with 2 or 3 spaces.

NAME AND ADDRESS HEADING

This consists of:

1. Your name—in capital letters, bolded, and in the largest typeface proportional to the rest of the resume.
2. Your address—It is acceptable to use your office or home address or both. Because your office address is at the top of the resume, it calls attention to your current institution which can be to your advantage (see sample resume for

Roberta Lieberman). However, if receiving correspondence at your office is a problem (and you never know who might open your mail), use only your home address.

3. Your home and office phone numbers. Omit the office number if a call from a prospective employer would be embarrassing at your current job.

4. You may want to include your Internet address if you have a home account; resist the temptation to use a workplace account. First, there are ethical issues about personal use of office systems. Second, network administrators or others frequently have access to all office accounts, and you may not care to have your personal mail scrutinized in this manner.

Let's see what Janet's heading looks like:

JANET F. TAYLOR
27 Chelsea Court
Woodland Springs, AR 72764
Home: (501) 555–2828 Office: (501) 555–1415
e-mail: jtaylor@aol.com

THE JOB OBJECTIVE

This statement is placed immediately under the heading and may be bolded. For instance, Janet's job objective appears like this:

Objective: Position as director in a small or medium-sized public library.

Don't forget, this statement is concise and to the point!

QUALIFICATIONS HEADING

This section will use one of the following headings: Summary of Qualifications, Highlights of Qualifications, or simply, Qualifications. There should be no more than five statements under this heading; they can be set off with bullets. Janet's qualifications are presented this way:

SUMMARY OF QUALIFICATIONS
- Outstanding supervisory and administrative skills gained in dynamic, medium-sized public library.
- Extensive experience in evaluation and implementation of automated systems.
- Assisted in the management of a budget of over $4 million.
- Proven skills in government and community relations.

WORK EXPERIENCE HEADING

This heading will vary depending on which resume format you have chosen.

Chronological and Combination Formats

With the chronological and combination formats, it is generally best to use these headings: Experience, Work Experience, or Work History.

When using chronological and combination formats, list the following:

1. job title
2. dates of employment; omit months—this information is generally irrelevant and clutters the resume
3. name of library or organization and location

Since Janet has chosen the combination format, she has listed her positions, the appropriate functional headings under each position, and one-liners (developed in Step 4) to support each heading (see Figure 4.1). In writing this part, she is constantly checking to make sure each one-liner relates to her job objective.

In a chronological or combination resume, be selective in the number of jobs that you list with one-liner descriptions. There is no set rule on how far back you should list employment; instead, include only those jobs that support your objective. If you feel it is important to list earlier positions, do so in summary form under an "Additional Work Experience" heading. Janet could list earlier experience like this:

ADDITIONAL WORK EXPERIENCE

- Reference Librarian, San Angelo Free Public Library, 1984–87.
- Elementary School Librarian, Sam Houston Elementary School, Eagle Pass, TX, 1982–84.

Functional Format

Now let's turn to the functional resume. Use one of the following headings: Experience, Skills and Experience, or Skills and Accomplishments. Many examples of functional formats are included in the resume examples. If this format is used, a "Work History" or "Work Experience" section should appear after the functional headings and one-liners. Had Janet chosen this format, her work history would have looked like that in Figure 4.2.

Figure 4.1 Janet Taylor's Work Experience in Combination Format

WORK EXPERIENCE

Redford County Public Library District, Redford, AR
Assistant Director, 1991—present

Management
- Assisted in daily management and administration of over 100 staff.
- Coordinated transition team to move central library to new building.
- Chaired library building committee, developed strategic plan, and presented plan to library board.
- Wrote comprehensive supervisory manual and library disaster plan.
- Served as acting director, 1990.

Automation
- Planned and implemented installation of Dynix automated system.
- Led team that evaluated library automation systems and made recommendation that was accepted.

Community and government relations
- Designed and implemented ADA Strategic Plan.
- Represented library on Redford County Business Development Committee.
- Negotiated building plans with community review board.

Fiscal management
- Assisted in managing a budget of $4.5 million.
- Cochaired audit review committee.
- Proposed a budget (1994) that was passed on the first attempt by the library board.

Associate Librarian/Head of Technical Services, 1989–91

Management
- Managed all aspects of technical service department including acquisitions, serials, interlibrary loan, and cataloging functions.
- Supervised 7 staff members.
- Outstanding performance evaluation.

Cataloging and Automation
- Extensive use of OCLC and the Dynix automated library system.
- Experience with AACR2 and MARC formats.
- Extensive audiovisual cataloging.

Head of Reference, 1987–89
- Supervised a staff of 8 reference librarians and 4 library aides.
- Served on the collection development committee.
- Chaired committee on user access.
- Revised and improved library reference guide.
- Developed and monitored database budget.

Figure 4.2. Janet Taylor's Work Experience in Functional Format

WORK EXPERIENCE

Redford County Public Library District, Redford, AR
- Assistant Director, 1991–present
- Acting Director, 1990
- Associate Librarian/Head of Technical Services, 1989–91
- Head of Reference, 1987–89

San Angelo Free Public Library, San Angelo, TX
- Reference Librarian, 1984–87

Sam Houston Elementary School, Eagle Pass, TX
- School Librarian, 1982–84

EDUCATION HEADING

This heading generally appears simply as Education. Under it, list the following in reverse chronological order:

1. your degree
2. the school and location
3. year of degree
4. major
5. honors (cum laude, summa cum laude, etc.)

Generally, degree acronyms such as B.A., B.S., and M.A. are understood by most resume readers. For the nonlibrarian reader, however, you may want to list Master of Library Science as opposed to M.L.S. Do be consistent in either abbreviating or spelling out the degree. For degrees that are not commonly known, always spell them out—don't make the reader guess.

Janet's education is listed this way.

EDUCATION
M.S. in Library Science, University of North Texas, Denton, TX, 1982.
B.A., Grinnell College, Grinnell, IA, 1979. Major in psychology; minor in French.

PROFESSIONAL INVOLVEMENT HEADING

List professional organization involvement under one of the following headings: Professional Organizations, Professional Association Involvement, or Professional Activities. As we discussed earlier, don't just list memberships. If you have been actively involved in an association, be sure to indicate it. The functional format lends itself well to highlighting transferable skills and experience you have gained in professional associations.

Janet would list her activities in this style:

PROFESSIONAL ASSOCIATION INVOLVEMENT

American Library Association, 1987–present
- Supervisory Skills Committee, Library Administration and Management Association. Helped to establish a listserv on supervisory skills and assisted with the planning and implementation of annual conference program: "First Line Supervisors: On the Edge."

Arkansas Library Association, 1985–present
- Member, 50th Anniversary Committee. Served on a team that planned association events for celebration. This included a Tribute Day event involving Arkansas legislators and media.
- Secretary, 1989–90.

ADDITIONAL HEADINGS

If relevant, include the following headings: Awards or Honors, Publications, Presentations, and/or Research and Grant Activities.

Volunteer work and personal interests can be listed as Volunteer Work, Volunteer Activities, Volunteer Experience, Personal Interests, Personal Activities, Volunteer Work/Personal Interests, or Other Activities.

Janet decided that volunteer work and personal interests should be included:

VOLUNTEER WORK/PERSONAL INTERESTS
- Reading is Fun program volunteer, 1989–90. Tutored elementary school children on weekends.
- Volunteer coordinator, St. Mary Parish, 1992. Organized volunteer visits to three nursing and long-term care facilities.
- Embroidery, roller blading, travel, French language group.

STEP 8: HOW THE RESUME LOOKS

Up to this point we have dealt primarily with the *substance* of the resume. Now it's time to examine how it *looks*. Well-tailored language won't mean a thing if the resume doesn't have curbside appeal, i.e., an attractive format that is easy-to-read. In this section, we will consider the following elements to ensure that your resume looks visually appealing:

- resume length
- formats and PC tips for graphics
- paper

Finally, we will take a look at Janet Taylor's finished product.

HOW LONG SHOULD YOUR RESUME BE?

This is one of the most debated questions of the ages. One page? Two pages? Three or longer? Everyone seems to have a different perspective. There is no hard and fast rule—each individual is different, and so is a resume. A one-page resume is ideal—the reader can quickly review it and capture the "big picture." Don't limit yourself to one page, however, if it means that you must reduce the margins to the point where there is no white space on the page or the type font becomes so minuscule that you need a magnifying glass to read it. That said, depending on your background, experience, and career level, one page simply will not be enough in many cases. Generally speaking, a two-page resume will not cost you any points. In the event that your resume pages become separated, be sure to put your name on the second page. But do think carefully before you go to a third page; review carefully to make sure every element is absolutely necessary. Remember that your resume may be one of several hundred being reviewed and the employer will spend only seconds with it.

One exception to this rule is the Curriculum Vitae (CV), which is more popular and often required in academic institutions. The CV will include detailed information about publications, courses taught, and the like, and therefore requires greater length. An example of a CV is included in the sample resume chapters.

USING THE PC TO CREATE THE PERFECT FORMAT

Let's start off with some guidelines to give your format a professional appearance:

- Use "bullets" for lists—they create a clear, graphic image and are easy-to-follow.
- Put headings in **bold**. This makes it easier for the eye to move from one section to the next.
- Make sure you have lots of **white** space on the pages. Don't shrink your margins and fill every inch of the paper with text. Leaving white space makes it easier to read.

- When it comes to a typeface, choose one that is traditional and conservative, simple and dignified. Avoid script, old English, or any "creative" typeface. *Italics* can be useful for headings and for names of journals, but use these features with restraint. Vary the typeface as little as possible. Type size should be easily readable—resist the temptation to use small type.

Now, take some time to review the sample resumes included in this book in chapters 5–9. You will observe various styles of format and organization, each of which gives a distinctive look, yet is easy-to-read and visually pleasing. Again, you don't need fancy desktop publishing or graphics packages to achieve a professional look. All of the resumes in these chapters were completed on my home computer using WordPerfect. The optional disk available for this book contains these resumes which you can now adapt to more easily create your own resume.

In reviewing the sample resumes, you will note the use of graphic lines, *italics*, and **bold** to add visual appeal. The lines were created using one of these WordPerfect 5.1 options:

- *Screen* (Ctrl F3) to create horizontal single and double bar lines
- *Graphics* (Alt F9) to create vertical and horizontal lines of varying widths

Use graphic features sparingly, and remember that too many graphics can detract from the content of the resume. For positions requiring an artistic bent, something more creative may be appropriate, but use novel or unique formats with great caution. The goal is to find just the right balance.

PAPER

Consult a good stationery store for a good selection of paper. The one you choose should:

- be of good quality
- be white or cream color; *never* use colored paper—it looks unprofessional and will not photocopy well should the resume reader decide to share it with someone else.
- have significant cotton content and a hard finish, a nice feel and heft; avoid textured papers since print quality may be uneven with certain types of printers
- have, if possible, a matching envelope, $8^1/_2 \times 11$", to allow you to send the resume without folding it.

Use a good quality laser printer, not a dot matrix, if possible. Avoid photocopying a resume and resist faxing it. Remember that the employer may show it to someone else, and a fax doesn't make the best presentation. If a potential employer needs it quickly, use an overnight delivery service. Don't use doublesided copies for resumes—the reader may neglect to turn it over.

Now let's take a look at how Janet's final resume turned out (see Figure 4.3).

This is quite a contrast to Janet's original resume! All of the problems we originally noted have been addressed. The look is crisp and professional, and uses some graphic lines to add visual interest. She has also included her name at the top of page 2 in the event the pages become separated.

STEP 9: JUST WHEN YOU THINK YOU'RE DONE: A FINAL CHECKLIST

Whew! You've come a long way. Before you turn it over to your potential employer, though, let's review the following checklist to make sure it is picture perfect:

1. Proofread—check and recheck grammar, spelling, and punctuation.
2. Is it neat? Coffee rings and potato chip stains don't belong here.
3. Time out for a reality check. One of the best ways to put the finishing touches on your resume is to have someone else review it. Choose among the following individuals to give you this critical feedback:

   - peers
   - mentors
   - managers
   - someone who doesn't know you well; you'll often get the most valuable insights here
   - someone who hires in the field of your job objective
   - someone outside of the field of librarianship—they will be quick to question vague language or unfamiliar acronyms
   - if you are an unsuccessful candidate for a job and have an opportunity to follow up with the interviewer, ask for suggestions on how your resume can be improved

---

Figure 4.3. Janet Taylor's Final Resume

JANET F. TAYLOR
27 Chelsea Court
Woodland Springs, AR 72764
Home: (501)555–2828 Office: (501)555–1415
e-mail: jtaylor@aol.com

Objective: Position as Director in a small or medium-sized public library.

SUMMARY OF QUALIFICATIONS

- Outstanding supervisory and administrative skills gained in dynamic, medium-sized public library.
- Extensive experience in evaluation and implementation of automated systems.
- Assisted in managing a budget of over $4 million.
- Proven skills in government and community relations.

WORK EXPERIENCE

Redford County Public Library District, Redford, AR

Assistant Director, 1991–present

Management
- Assisted in daily management and administration of over 100 staff.
- Coordinated transition team to move central library to new building.
- Chaired library building committee, developed strategic plan, and presented plan to the library board.
- Wrote comprehensive supervisory manual and library disaster plan.
- Served as acting director, 1990.

Automation
- Planned and implemented installation of Dynix automated system.
- Led team which evaluated library automation systems and made recommendation that was accepted.

Community and government relations
- Designed and implemented ADA Strategic Plan.
- Represented library on Redford County Business Development Committee.
- Negotiated building plans with community review board.

Fiscal management
- Assisted in managing a budget of $4.5 million.
- Cochaired Audit Review Committee.
- Proposed a budget (1994) that was passed on the first attempt by the library board.

Associate Librarian/Head of Technical Services, 1989–91

Management
- Managed all aspects of technical service department including acquisitions, serials, interlibrary loan, and cataloging functions.
- Supervised 7 staff members.
- Outstanding performance evaluation.

Janet Taylor, p. 2.

Associate Librarian continued

Cataloging and Automation
- Extensive use of OCLC and the Dynix automated library system.
- Experience with AACR2 and MARC formats.
- Extensive audiovisual cataloging.

Head of Reference, 1987–89
- Supervised a staff of 8 reference librarians and 4 library aides.
- Served on the collection development committee.
- Chaired committee on user access.
- Revised and improved library reference guide.
- Developed and monitored database budget.

ADDITIONAL WORK EXPERIENCE

Reference Librarian, San Angelo Free Public Library, 1984–87.
Elementary School Librarian, Sam Houston Elementary School, Eagle Pass, TX, 1982–84.

EDUCATION

M.S. in Library Science, University of North Texas, Denton, TX, 1982.

B.A., Grinnell College, Grinnell, IA, 1979. Major in psychology; minor in French. Member of debate team and oratory choir.

PROFESSIONAL ASSOCIATION INVOLVEMENT

American Library Association, 1987–present
- Supervisory Skills Committee, Library Administration and Management Association. Helped to establish a listserv on supervisory skills and assisted with the planning and implementation of annual conference program: "First Line Supervisors: On the Edge."

Arkansas Library Association, 1985–present
- Member, 50th Anniversary Committee. Served on a team that planned association events for celebration. This included a Tribute Day event involving Arkansas legislators and media.
- Secretary, 1989–90.

VOLUNTEER WORK/PERSONAL INTERESTS

- Reading is Fun program volunteer, 1989–90. Tutored elementary school children on weekends.
- Volunteer coordinator, St. Mary Parish, 1992. Organized volunteer visits to three nursing and long-term care facilities.
- Embroidery, roller blading, travel, French language group.

4. Have you described your positions in your own words? Avoided phrases like "duties included" or "responsible for"? Using language from formal job descriptions is not acceptable.
5. Have you included relevant nonprofessional work experience and volunteer work? Don't underestimate these when they are germane to your job objective.
6. Have you accounted for periods of unemployment? Remember that resume readers are always alert to this.
7. Have you used acronyms that will have no meaning for the employer? Only use those that are universally known.
8. Will your resume pass the *New York Times* test? In other words, have you written anything you wouldn't want published on the front page of a newspaper?
9. Is your resume concise and to the point?
10. Is there plenty of white space? Is it easy-to-read?
11. Have you checked and rechecked to make sure that every statement in your resume supports your job objective?
12. Have you carefully proofed for typos? Do not make handwritten corrections!

If you have answered "yes" to all of the above questions, you have produced the job-winning resume. Congratulations!

SAMPLE RESUMES AND DISK: AN INTRODUCTION

Now let's turn to samples. The next five chapters provide you with a wide range of sample resumes of "real life" librarians (with names and places changed). They have been organized in broad categories of target positions:

- automation/systems librarians (management and nonmanagement)
- librarian (nonmanagement)
- librarian (supervisory/management)
- library school student (recent graduate)
- special librarian

Each chapter includes the following:

- special tips on that particular job category
- a listing by name of each resume, a description of the individual's job objective, and background on the position for which they are applying
- details about how the individual tailored their resume, special techniques they used, why they chose one format over another, and other unique features
- copies of the actual resumes

The examples have been chosen because they represent many different types of your target libraries and organizations, such as academic, public, school, association, private companies, foundations, and government agencies. They also represent individuals at many different career stages, with each resume tailored for a position in a particular job category. Remember that many of the individuals have written their resumes to target jobs in different areas of librarianship. For example, in the Automation/Systems Librarian chapter, a librarian in a government agency seeks a position in an academic library.

The templates of resumes on the disk are formatted in WordPerfect 5.1, which correspond to the last name of the samples in the book text; resumes can be found in directories that correspond to the appropriate chapter. These examples are intended to provide you with inspiration, and none will resemble your resume exactly. So, customize the template that best suits your needs.

5 AUTOMATION/SYSTEMS LIBRARIAN (MANAGEMENT AND NONMANAGEMENT)— SAMPLE RESUMES

In this chapter we'll take a look at four individuals who are applying for automation/systems librarian positions, a burgeoning and exciting area of librarianship. Employers are naturally looking for people who have specific knowledge of various databases, systems, and networks. While this specialized knowledge is extremely valuable, so too is the ability to be flexible and adaptable to an environment that is constantly reinventing itself. It is important to document skills that demonstrate your ability to adjust to change and to be aggressive in seeking out new trends, solutions, and products.

Here are some other tips to keep in mind when writing resumes for these types of positions:

1. Be especially wary of system acronyms. While many acronyms are well-known (MARC, OCLC, UNIX, NEXIS, etc.) in the profession, others are more obscure. When in doubt, spell it out or describe it so the employer won't have to guess.
2. Don't simply indicate that you have "knowledge of" a particular system. In describing your experience with a system, ask yourself these questions:
   - Were you involved in the planning stage of the system? For example, did you serve on or head a committee to look at the feasibility of installing a network?
   - Did you work with vendors in the planning or implementation stage? How extensive was your involvement?
   - Did you receive training on this system? Did you receive any type of certification?

- Did you work with users directly? Did you plan or implement training? Did you do a survey? A feasibility study? A cost analysis? Did you prepare a report?

3. Define your accomplishments in terms of results. How did your automation solution improve service, enhance operations, streamline a process, or save time?
4. Be sure to emphasize the "human element." A frequent criticism of automation staff is that while they may have excellent technical abilities, they don't have adequate people skills. If you have led committees or worked closely with users, be sure to indicate that. Emphasize any significant work that you did in surveying users or getting feedback.

With that said, let's meet our candidates.

Vanessa Hilton is looking for a position as head of systems in a large public or academic library. Although she has published and spoken extensively, she is selective in choosing publications and presentations so as to limit her resume to two pages. She chooses the chronological format to emphasize her current position as Assistant Head of Systems (see Figure 5.1). Note the italicized headings.

Valerie Hinjosa has served in three positions in one organization. They have involved progressively more responsibility and reinforced her job goal: a position as a university electronic information resources librarian. Her one-liner statements are very focused on supporting her job objective (see Figure 5.2).

Gerry Kinsey seeks a position as a director for systems in a large university. She has a good range of experience in several different jobs and chooses the chronological format to market herself (see Figure 5.3). Note that Gerry defines lesser known acronyms, like DELNET, that are not readily identifiable to most employers.

Russell Moyers has just lost his job as a senior manager of an information center due to the abolishment of a state agency. His goal is to find a similar position in the private sector. His job progression in the agency was impressive and he developed solid skills. To highlight these attributes, he chooses the chronological format (see Figure 5.4). His qualifications statement is especially well-written.

Figure 5.1. Sample Resume—Vanessa Hilton

Vanessa Hilton

Home: 671 West Avenue, Bismarck, ND 89443; 607–555–1415
Office: University of North Dakota, Library, Bismarck, ND 89432; 607–555–3232

Objective: A position as head of systems in a large public or academic library.

Summary of Qualifications

- Extensive systems experience in libraries.
- Experience working with automation vendors.
- Background in automation planning and implementation.
- Experienced in all areas of administration including budget and staff training.

Professional Experience

Assistant Head of Systems, University of North Dakota Library, Bismarck, ND, 1988 to present.
- Assisted with planning, installation, and implementation of an online catalog system.
- Resolved all equipment and software problems, including PCs, e-mail, and IBM mainframe applications.
- Performed a system analysis study on gift acquisitions and bindery functions.
- Developed a UNIX-based network menu front-end system, a library gopher, and an online catalog.
- Designed, implemented, and taught the staff training program for a new online catalog.
- Assisted in the supervision of 6 systems staff.

Acting Budget Officer, University of North Dakota, 1994 to 1995
- Administered and managed a $5.6 million budget.
- Automated internal budget processing and developed new budgeting model.

American Library Association International Library Fellow, National Library, Estonia, 1993 to 1994 (six months).
- Advised on automation for the country's public library system.
- Helped develop a five-year automation plan.
- Advised on the selection of MARC record-creation hardware and software and Novell network.
- Introduced the Internet including e-mail, gophers, and World Wide Web.

Library System Intern, University of Hawaii, Honolulu, HI, 1984 to 1985.
- Assisted with the development of a staff and user training program for the new online catalog system.
- Performed OCLC data entry.
- Assisted with Dialog searches and PC software training in the Graduate School's PC Lab.

Education

M.L.S., University of Hawaii, Honolulu, HI, 1985.
B.S., Physics, University of Hawaii, Honolulu, HI, 1983.
Continuing Education: Earned 12 credits in University of North Dakota M.P.A. program, 1990; courses included statistics, research methodology, ethics, and organizational theory.

Honors

- Recipient, 3M/Junior Members Round Table Professional Development Grant, 1984.
- Beta Phi Mu (Library of Science Honorary Society), University of Hawaii, 1984.
- Alumni Scholarship, University of Hawaii School of Library and Information Studies, 1985.

Selected Presentations

- Keynote address to the Library Association of Estonia, 1994.
- "Your Guide to the Internet," presented at University of North Dakota Library Conference, August 1995.
- "Library Networking in the '90s," a paper presented at the North Dakota Council of Higher Education Computer Services Conference, 1996.

Selected Publications

- Numerous book reviews for *Information Technology in Libraries* and *Library Journal*.
- Editor, Newsletter, North Dakota Library Association, 1995 to present.
- "Online Resources in North Dakota's Libraries," a series of four articles published in the *North Dakota Library Association Newsletter*, 1995.

Professional Activities

- Chair, North Dakota Library Association Local Arrangements Committee, 1996 Annual Conference.
- Chair, North Dakota Consortium of Academic Library's Automation Task Force, 1993 to present.
- President, Hawaii's Student Chapter of the American Society of Information Science, 1985.

Figure 5.2. Sample Resume—Valerie Hinjosa

Valerie C. Hinjosa

1710 Valley Vista Highway #B-2
Oakland, CA 95001
Office: 408-555-1393 Home: 408-555-8888
e-mail: hinjosav@aol.com

Objective: To serve as Electronic Information Resources Librarian at the University Library, University of California, Santa Cruz.

Summary of Qualifications

- Experience in planning and implementing technology in a library.
- Strong communication and organizational skills.
- Excellent knowledge of a wide range of online services.
- Extensive experience working in a scientific environment.

Work Experience

California Department of Health, San Francisco, CA.

Technical Information Specialist, 1995–present.
- Researched and responded to reference inquiries from state health officials.
- Monitored health-related legislation in the California Assembly.
- Performed extensive online searches specializing in health databases.
- Attended and reviewed state Assembly committee meetings on health issues.

Public Information Specialist, 1994.
- Responded to over 50 public inquiries each day, primarily by telephone.
- Assigned requests to health specialists within the Department of Health.
- Served on committee that implemented a network.

Serials Technician, 1993.
- Assisted in the conversion of automated serials control system from Faxon Manager to Microlinx.
- Created database records, tracked serial receipts, and performed software maintenance.

Systems Librarian, Texas Woman's University, Denton, TX, 1992.
- Maintained ProCite database of 1180 rare (pre-1850) titles.
- Performed extensive online and Internet searches.
- Installed and maintained library software.
- Managed monograph and serial acquisitions.
- Wrote and edited grant proposals for library funding.

Freelance Work

Writer and Translator, 1989–94.
- Wrote film/theater reviews and natural history articles.
- Edited community events and entertainment calendars.
- Created brochures and flyers.
- Translated news features from English into Spanish, French, and German.

Courseware Consultant, 1993. Kodak International Center for Training and Management Development, Rochester, NY.
- Designed and developed telecommunications training package for marketing representatives.
- Supervised staff of 3 programmers.

Professional Associations

Special Libraries Association
- Treasurer, Student Chapter, Texas Woman's University.
- Member, Student Affiliation and Scholarship Committee.
- Member, Pamphlet Task Force, Natural History Caucus.

Education

M.A. in Library Science, Texas Woman's University, Denton, TX, 1991. Received Beta Mu Scholarship.

B.A., University of Tennessee, Knoxville, TN, 1989. Magna cum laude, Phi Beta Kappa. Major in Spanish. Coursework at the Universidad Complutense de Madrid.

Figure 5.3. Sample Resume—Gerry Kinsey

GERRY KINSEY
Division of Library Development and Services
Delaware Department of Education
Wilmington, DE 43101
607-555-3245

JOB OBJECTIVE: Systems Director for the Library, University of Oklahoma.

QUALIFICATIONS

- Expert knowledge of networks and networked environments.
- Experienced in coordinating electronic services in a university environment.
- Administrative and supervisory experience.
- Excellent skills in strategic planning.

WORK EXPERIENCE

Assistant Director, Delaware Department of Education, Division of Library Development and Services, Wilmington, DE, 1994–present.

- Facilitated the development and evaluation of DELNET, Delaware's Online Information Network.
- Consulted with libraries and state and local agencies in making their resources available.
- Served as state coordinator and liaison to public library directors.
- Provided access for over 30 new online resources in 1995.
- Served on Department of Education Automation Strategic Planning Committee.

Coordinator, Electronic Reference Services, University of Delaware, Newark, DE, 1990–94.

- Administered university Computer Assisted Research and Automated Reference Services Division.
- Managed collection development and budgeting for electronic resources in all disciplines.
- Supervised 10 librarians.
- Developed policies and procedures for the division.
- Served as liaison with faculty.

Librarian, Headquarters Library, DuPont, Inc., Wilmington, DE, 1989–90.

- Provided extensive reference to headquarters and 4 corporate libraries.
- Responded to over 50 reference requests each day.
- Managed acquisitions and original cataloging for all corporate libraries.

EDUCATION

M.L.S., Queens College, City University of New York, Flushing, NY, 1987.

B.A. in Political Science, University of Virginia, Charlottesville, VA, 1985.

PUBLICATIONS

Frequent reviewer for *Government Information Quarterly.*

"Best CD-ROMs of 1995," *CD-ROM World*, 8 (June 1995).

"International Online Information Meeting Review," *Library Hi-Tech News*, March 1994.

PRESENTATIONS

"Managing Technology in Public Libraries," Library Executive Leadership Institute, Newark, DE, 1995. Coordinated one-day seminar.

"Stop the Madness: Print vs. Electronic Resources," panelist at program of Association for Library Collections and Technical Services, American Library Association, Annual Conference, 1994.

PROFESSIONAL INVOLVEMENT

Special Interest Group for CD-ROM Applications and Technology (SIGNAT)
- CD-ROM Consistent Interface Committee, member, 1990–92.
- Library Information Technology Committee, cochair, 1994–95.

Delaware Library Association
- Treasurer, 1994–95. Streamlined accounting procedures and budget recommendation procedures.

American Association of University Women
- Diversity Task Force Chair, Delaware Chapter, 1993–present.

OUTSIDE ACTIVITIES

- Participate in running marathons and triathlons. Placed second in age group, "Run for the Cure" race, 1994.

- Costume Director, Little Theater of Wilmington, 1993–95.

Figure 5.4. Sample Resume—Russell Moyers

RUSSELL L. MOYERS
3701 Washington Square #315
Baltimore, MD 20555-2678
301-555-9292
E-MAIL: rmoye@aol.com

CAREER OBJECTIVE: A senior position in information services or management using proven administrative skills to increase and improve the productivity of a library.

SUMMARY OF QUALIFICATIONS

- Expertise and leadership skills in managing an automated information center.
- Over 14 years of experience in developing staff and resources in information services.
- Extensive experience in implementing new technologies.
- Strong communication skills.

PROFESSIONAL EXPERIENCE

Maryland Department of Technology Research

Manager, Information Services, 1990–present.
- Supervised staff of 8 (including 4 librarians).
- Answered over 1,400 requests a month.
- Prepared and monitored $325K budget for all salary and materials.
- Provided reference services in a networked IBM environment.
- Evaluated and implemented new technologies, including Internet CD-ROM.
- Hired and trained all personnel.
- Served as network supervisor in a Novell LAN environment.

Assistant Manager, Information Services, 1983–1990.
- Coordinated all reference services.
- Supervised and performed online searches using Dialog, MEDLARS, NEXIS/LEXIS, Dow Jones, Legi-Slate.
- Supervised Interlibrary Loan system and electronic mail.
- Assisted in development and maintenance of automated acquisitions, catalog, and circulation systems.
- Maintained and interpreted statistics (Lotus 1-2-3) for management reports.
- Indexed and abstracted Department of Technology Research reports for inclusion in NTIS database.
- Trained department staff on online services to improve productivity.

National Oil and Gas Institute, Washington, DC, 1980–83.

Information Specialist
- Performed wide range of reference services to staff and members of the association.
- Acquired excellent knowledge of technical and business information sources.
- Coordinated publication of Institute calendar and Information Directory.

ADDITIONAL WORK EXPERIENCE

University of Maryland, Terrapin Library, College Park, MD.
- Librarian, Acquisitions/Serials Department, 1979-80.
- Librarian, Information Services Department, 1980.

AT&T Laboratories Technical Library, Burtonsville, MD.
- Reference Intern, 1979.

EDUCATION

Certificate of Completion, Special Libraries Association Middle Management units in Management Skills, Marketing and Public Relations, Human Resources, and Analytical Tools, 1994.

Master of Library Science, College of Library and Information Services, University of Maryland, College Park, MD, 1980.

Bachelor of Science in Biology, Radcliffe College, Cambridge, MA, 1976.

PROFESSIONAL AFFILIATIONS

Member: American Library Association, Special Libraries Association.

6 LIBRARIAN (NONSUPERVISORY)— SAMPLE RESUMES

This chapter presents resumes of individuals seeking nonsupervisory librarian positions. Graphics in these resumes are distinctive yet understated. They catch the reader's eye, but don't overwhelm.

Some tips for these types of positions:

1. When subject expertise is required, be sure to cover yours in the qualification bullets or highlight it in the work summary. Mention any experience with specialized databases or the range of systems in which you have expertise.
2. For reference librarian positions, emphasize oral communication skills. Employers are always looking for candidates who can interact well with a wide range of people, so consider this element carefully.

Paula Carrillo is seeking a position as an assistant librarian/science reference librarian in a university library. The announcement for this position specifically states that the job requires an academic degree or extensive experience in science; demonstrated knowledge of electronic information resources; and excellent oral and written communication skills. Since Paula has good experience in each of these areas, she chooses a functional format and tailors those headings to demonstrate her skill areas (see Figure 6.1). Her work history is not extensive, so she includes a nonprofessional position—the stamina required for the reference desk is not unlike that needed for waiting tables.

Judith Fontaine is seeking a position as a government information data librarian in a public library system. Note that Judith's resume is only one page; she is focused and delivers an excellent presentation that can be quickly read (see Figure 6.2). She effectively cites her professional activities in the qualifications section.

Kenneth Lanahan is applying for a position as a life sciences librarian. Note how carefully he has written his one-liner statements; all reinforce his job objective (see Figure 6.3). He has also emphasized his subject expertise in the qualifications section.

Joseph Walker's goal is be a catalog librarian. His work experience is directly relevant to his targeted position, so he chooses a chronological format (see Figure 6.4).

Figure 6.1. Sample Resume—Paula Carrillo

PAULA R. CARRILLO
12 Old Mill Road
Richmond, VA 22215
Home: (804) 555-1270 Office: (804) 555-4319

OBJECTIVE	Assistant Librarian/Science Reference Librarian, Louisiana State University
QUALIFICATIONS	Reference experience with extensive science background. Proven writing and speaking abilities. Experienced searcher with electronic information resources. Ability to juggle multiple demands in high-pressure environment.
EXPERIENCE	Science Reference • Provided in-person and telephone reference to students and faculty. • Knowledge of wide range of science sources. • Prepared bibliographies for faculty for curriculum development. • Evaluated science reference sources for professional recognition. Electronic Information Sources • Routinely used databases related to science reference including MEDLINE. • Experienced Internet searcher. • Assisted in database budget planning. • Evaluated a wide range of electronic sources for possible acquisition. Writing and Speaking • Wrote circulation procedures manual. • Conducted classes for students on use of CD-ROM databases. • Gave tours of library to visitors.
WORK HISTORY	1993–present Reference Librarian, Library, Medical College of Virginia, Richmond, VA. 1992–93 Circulation Clerk, National Library of Medicine, Bethesda, MD. 1991–92 Waitress (part-time), Bon Temps Bar & Grill, New Orleans, LA.
EDUCATION	Master of Arts, School of Library and Information Science, Louisiana State University, Baton Rouge, LA, 1991. Bachelor of Arts in Physics, Bryn Mawr College, Bryn Mawr, PA, 1989.
PROFESSIONAL INVOLVEMENT	Special Libraries Association • Bulletin Editor, Science and Technology Division, 1994–95. Created popular new column called "Science Reference Exchange." • Membership Committee, Nuclear Science Division, 1993–94.
OTHER ACTIVITIES	Sports: Tennis, swimming, biking. National High School Chess Association: Coach students on competitive play and serve as judge in contests.

Figure 6.2 Sample Resume—Judith Fontaine

Judith Fontaine
1244 E. 19th Avenue
Dallas, TX 34103
Office: 214–555–2433

OBJECTIVE

Government Information Data Librarian, Dallas Public Library.

QUALIFICATIONS

- Wide range of experience in delivering government data.
- Extensive database searching skills.
- Entire library career devoted to providing technical data to a variety of clients.
- Active professional involvement in activities related to delivery of government information.

WORK EXPERIENCE

Technical Information Specialist, Texas Department of Transportation, Dallas, TX, 1994–present.
- Maintained library for state agency that provides data to other state agencies and local governments.
- Used a wide range of software packages to deliver statistical information.
- Provided microcomputer support to library and statistical units.
- Compiled annual report of Texas transportation statistics.

Economics Librarian, Management and Social Sciences Library, University of Texas, Dallas, TX, 1992–94.
- Provided business and economic reference to students and faculty.
- Searched on many different databases related to economics.
- Served as liaison to economics department.
- Developed and implemented orientation sessions for new economics department students.

Library Assistant, AMIGOS Bibliographic Council, Inc., Dallas, TX, 1991–92.
- Assisted in the development of training materials.
- Provided telephone reference and trouble-shooting assistance.
- Knowledge of cataloging rules, MARC formats, and OCLC online systems.

EDUCATION

Master of Library and Information Science, the University of Texas at Austin, Austin, TX, 1992.

Bachelor of Arts, Economics, University of Idaho, Moscow, ID, 1990.

PROFESSIONAL ACTIVITIES

Special Libraries Association
- Chair, Transportation Section, 1994–95. Coordinated publication of SLA bibliography on transportation sources.

Texas Library Association
- Member, Networking Committee, 1993–94.

Figure 6.3. Sample Resume—Kenneth Lanahan

Kenneth Lanahan

84 Oak Court #C-1
Knoxville, TN 03210
704-555-9415
E-MAIL: LANAHAN@aol.com

Objective: To work as Librarian (Life Sciences) in Sciences Library, Antioch College.

Qualifications

- Extensive background in science librarianship.
- Experienced in working in fast-paced academic library.
- Broad knowledge of science databases.
- Ability to easily juggle multiple demands.
- Graduate degree in zoology.

Work Summary

User Education/Reference Librarian and Life Sciences Bibliographer

Science Library, University of Tennessee, Knoxville, TN, 1993–present.

- Coordinated all user education activities.
- Selected, trained, and supervised student assistants.
- Scheduled reference desk and user education classes.
- Consulted with faculty on life sciences sources and online services.
- Provided general reference in Science Library.

Librarian

Information Center, MEF Corporation, Iowa City, IA, 1992–93.

- Provided reference service to staff of 50 scientists.
- Performed searches using a variety of databases with particular emphasis on life sciences.
- Provided troubleshooting for microcomputers.
- Compiled current awareness bibliographies for scientists.

Library Intern

Library, Long Island University, Brookville, NY, 1991–92.

- Gave library tours to new students and faculty.
- Performed OCLC data entry.
- Provided reference service and completed database searches.

Education

- M.S., Library Science, Long Island University, Brookville, NY, 1992.
- M.A., Zoology, University at Albany, State University of New York, 1989.
- B.S., Science, St. John's University, Jamaica, NY, 1986.

Publications

- *Science Libraries: Focus on Technology*, Occasional Paper #6, Special Libraries Association, 1995.

Professional Activities

Special Libraries Association
- Chair-Elect, Biological Sciences Division, 1995–96.

American Library Association
- Member, Association of College and Research Libraries, Forum on Science and Technology Library Research, 1994–95.

Figure 6.4. Sample Resume—Joseph R. Walker

Joseph R. Walker

931 W. 60th Ave.
Portland, OR 91110
Office: 612–555–2929

OBJECTIVE: **To work as a Catalog Librarian.**

HIGHLIGHTS OF QUALIFICATIONS

- Excellent knowledge of cataloging principles and procedures including AACR2.
- Experience in training staff in cataloging procedures.
- Working knowledge of several languages.
- Experience with print and nonprint formats.

WORK EXPERIENCE

Serials/GPO Records Librarian, Eastern Washington University Libraries, Cheney, WA, 1993 to present.

- Planned and directed acquisition, control, and cataloging of serials.
- Served as SuDocs liaison.
- Maintained bibliographic, holdings, control, and retention records for U.S. government publications.
- Trained staff in technical services unit.
- Expert knowledge of AACR2, MARC, LCSH, LCCS, and SuDocs classification and depository requirements.

Catalog Clerk, Library, University of Tennessee, Knoxville, TN, 1991–92.

- Assisted in original cataloging, classification, and authority work for materials in all formats.
- Assisted with OCLC Enhance programs.
- Completed preparatory cataloging for French and Spanish materials.
- Received Superior Performance rating.

EDUCATION

M.S. in Library Science, University of Tennessee, Knoxville, TN, 1991.

B.A., Spanish, University of Puerto Rico, San Juan, PR, 1989. Graduated *cum laude*.

LANGUAGES

Fluent in Spanish and French. Able to read German and Portuguese. Studied in Barcelona for three months while working on B.A.

Joseph R. Walker
Page 2

PROFESSIONAL AND OUTSIDE ACTIVITIES

Association for Library Collections and Technical Services (American Library Association)
- Member, Digital Resources Committee, 1995–96. Helping to plan program for next annual conference, Digital Resources: The CD-ROM of Tomorrow.

Special Libraries Association
- Member, Affirmative Action Committee, 1994–95.

7 LIBRARIAN (SUPERVISORY/ MANAGEMENT)— SAMPLE RESUMES

This chapter turns to supervisory/management positions. Here are some resume pointers for these types of positions:

1. Demonstrate that you are results oriented—i.e., clearly identify your accomplishments. Demonstrate how you have improved service, streamlined operations, saved money, implemented a system that solved problems, and so forth.
2. In addition to routine management duties, be sure to include any relevant leadership activities that you may have performed on an ad hoc basis. For example, have you led a committee? What did the committee produce? Did you write a report? Were the recommendations implemented? Don't overlook any opportunity to demonstrate the *results* of any leadership activity in which you were engaged.
3. Indicate any temporary promotions or acting positions.
4. Include any leadership activities in professional or volunteer positions.

Here are our candidates:

James Atherton is currently head of reference at a large academic library. His current job objective is to obtain a position as an associate dean for a small or mid-sized university library. Because James has had progressively more responsible positions in one academic library and he wants to capitalize on the prestige of this institution, he chooses the chronological format (see Figure 7.1). Note how well he has quantified his accomplishments (number of students taught, number of staff supervised, etc.).

William Chin is currently head of public services in a major university library, and his career has steadily progressed in this institution. He now seeks a position with more responsibility and is applying for the head of a university science and technology library. Because he has been with one institution for a long time, he chooses the combination resume style to emphasize the broad range of skills he has acquired in several positions (see Figure 7.2).

Eliot Farnsworth is applying for a position as manager of technical services at a large university. His experience is excellent and he chooses the chronological format to highlight his relevant qualifications in his current position (see Figure 7.3).

Elizabeth Keller is a media coordinator in a medium-sized school district and seeks a progressively more responsible position in a larger system. Note her "Educational Philosophy" statement—this is slightly unconventional, but works well with her background and job objective (see Figure 7.4).

Constance MacPherson is a library science professor with a specialty in school library media. She has extensive teaching experience and has published widely. Her resume is a Curriculum Vitae—it contains comprehensive information on her speaking, publishing, and research activities (see Figure 7.5). The CV is generally used for academic positions. Note that Constance has not given a detailed description of all her positions, rather she has included positions from the last four years. Older positions are indicated in summary form. To emphasize her distinguished academic achievements, she has moved the "Education" section above "Work Experience."

Dean Myers is currently a branch manager in a large public library system. He would like to locate a position as assistant director of a small to medium-sized public library, and has employed the chronological format (see Figure 7.6).

Sally Walter is access services head in a large university. Her goal is to find a position as director of public services in a medium or large-sized university. Note how well she uses the combination resume to highlight her important skill areas (see Figure 7.7).

Figure 7.1. Sample Resume—James Atherton

James P. Atherton

---

12 Cutler Boulevard #107 • Berkeley, CA 94720-4600
Office: (510)555-4538 • E-mail: ather@aol.com

OBJECTIVE: Associate Dean in a small or medium-sized academic library.

SUMMARY OF QUALIFICATIONS

- Successfully administered complex reference activities in large university library.
- Developed innovative bibliographic instruction courses.
- Extensive background in collection development administration.
- Reputation for strong commitment to improving service for patrons.

WORK HISTORY

Undergraduate Library, University of California, Berkeley, CA

1993 to present
Head of Reference
- Coordinated all reference department activities including database services, government documents, bibliographic instruction, and outreach.
- Supervised 11 full-time and 5 part-time staff.
- Recruited, hired, and trained all reference staff.
- Planned and implemented all staff development activities.
- Developed library instruction class that combined online tutorials available through campus network with traditional tours.
- Coordinated all reference collection development.

1987 to 1993
History Reference Librarian and Outreach Coordinator
- Recommended books and periodicals for reference collection.
- Provided reference assistance to faculty, staff, and students.
- Instructed hundreds of students each semester on how to use the library.
- Taught "Introduction to Reference" in School of Library and Information Science.
- Implemented special library tours for local elementary schools.
- Served as Acting Bibliographic Instruction Coordinator, 1988.
- Supervised and wrote evaluations for reference interns.

University Archives, University of California at Berkeley, Berkeley, CA

1982
Archives Technician

- Reorganized student record microfilm collection.
- Designed online system for tracking microfilm loans.
- Designed more efficient shelving arrangement for collection.
- Wrote "Finding Guide to University Archives Microfilm."

James P. Atherton

Page 2

EDUCATION

M.L.S., School of Library and Information Studies, San Jose State University, San Jose, CA, 1980.

A.B.D., in History, University of Washington, Seattle.

Certificate in Archival Training, Columbia University, New York, NY, 1979.

M.A., History, Skidmore College, Saratoga Springs, NY, 1978.

B.A., French and History, Syracuse University, Syracuse, NY, 1974.

PROFESSIONAL ACTIVITIES

American Library Association
- Chair, Diversity Committee, Association of College and Research Libraries, 1994–95.
- Coordinator, Discussion Group—"Performance Issues for Reference/Information Librarians," Reference and Adult Services Division, 1993.

Organization of American Historians
- Member, Nominating Committee, 1995.
- Member, Archival Standards Committee, 1993–95.
    Coauthored "Archival Standards: A Review of the Past Decade," 1991.

OTHER ACTIVITIES

National Cystic Fibrosis Society
- Cochaired 10K Run, which raised over $ 40,000 in contributions.

Other interests include running, photography, paleontology, nature, conservation, drawing, and music.

Figure 7.2. Sample Resume—William Chin

WILLIAM F. CHIN
77 Beacon Hill • Boston, MA 02114-5824
Office: 617-555-4329

OBJECTIVE: To serve as Head of the Science and Technology Library, The University of Akron.

SUMMARY OF QUALIFICATIONS

* Experienced public services administrator in a science library.
* Broad knowledge of collection development in the sciences.
* Extensive experience with computer systems and electronic databases.
* Proven interpersonal skills with faculty, students, and staff.

WORK EXPERIENCE

Education and Science Library, Cabot Science Library, Harvard University, Cambridge, MA.

Head of Public Services, 1991–present.

Administration
* Coordinated and supervised circulation, reference, and processing staff in all public service activities.
* Led team that planned move of over 45,000 volumes to off-site storage.
* Managed public services budget.

Automation
* Planned and implemented the library's automated circulation system.
* Assisted in development of network.
* Evaluated science electronic services including full-text databases, CD-ROMs, and Internet resources.

Reference/Instruction Librarian and Psychology Specialist, 1988–91.

Reference
* Provided in-person reference in the field of psychology.
* Worked closely with faculty to develop course bibliographies and reserve collections.
* Scheduled reference desk and user education activities.

Collection Development
* Served as liaison to the psychology department for collection development.
* Reviewed psychology literature and publishers' catalogs to select material for the collection.
* Monitored the psychology book and serials fund.
* Team member on collection review committee to make decisions on weeding, storage, and journal selections.

TEACHING EXPERIENCE

Adjunct Faculty, Simmons College, Graduate School of Library and Information Science, Boston, MA. Taught the following courses:

- Bibliography: Theory and Technique, 1995.
- Information Resources and Libraries, 1992–94.
- Seminar in Science and Technology Reference, 1995.

ADDITIONAL WORK EXPERIENCE

Psychology Bibliographer	1984–88	Education and Science Library, Cabot Science Library, Harvard University
Reference Intern	1983–84	Graduate Library, Boston College

EDUCATION

M.L.S., Simmons College, Graduate School of Library and Information Sciences, Boston, MA, 1984.

Ph.D., Experimental Psychology, New York University, New York, NY, 1972. Dissertation: *Spreading Cortical Depression in Mice.*

M.A., Experimental Psychology, New York University, New York, NY, 1968.

B.S., Psychology, Vassar College, Poughkeepsie, NY, 1966. Graduated summa cum laude.

PUBLICATIONS

"Cognitive Styles—Practical Implications for Teaching Science," in *Learning to Teach—Instruction Workshops,* Association of College and Research Libraries, American Library Association, Chicago: 1991.

"Mentoring Science Students," *Special Libraries* 85, no. 4, Fall, 1994.

Frequent book review contributor to *Library Quarterly* and *Library Journal.*

Currently writing a book entitled *Emerging Technologies and the Library,* for Haworth Press.

PRESENTATIONS

"Comparing Modes of Instruction," ACRL Bibliographic Instruction and Research Sections and Library Instruction Round Table program: "Improve Instruction Through Evaluation," Philadelphia, 1995. Also facilitated group instruction.

"Developing a Library Instruction Program," New York Clearinghouse on Library Instruction Open House, February 4, 1994.

RESEARCH AND GRANT ACTIVITIES

- Recipient of Harvard University Office of Instructional Development Programs grant for development of a computer-assisted instruction program to teach undergraduate psychology students the organization of and access to journal material in the life sciences, 1992–93.

- National Science Foundation grant to support a study to compare and evaluate the effectiveness of computer-assisted instruction.

PROFESSIONAL ACTIVITIES

American Library Association

New Members Round Table
Chair, Nominating Committee, 1993–94.
Director for Membership, Awards and Continuing Education Committees, 1992–93.
EBSCO Scholarship Committee Chair, 1990–91.

Association of College and Research Libraries–Bibliographic Instruction Section
Learning to Teach Task Force, 1990–91.
Education for Bibliographic Instruction Committee, 1989–90.

Member: American Psychological Association, Medical Library Group of Massachusetts, Phi Beta Mu, Social and Behavioral Sciences Librarians Network.

Figure 7.3. Sample Resume—Eliot Farnsworth

Eliot T. Farnsworth
Swarthmore College Library
Swarthmore, PA 19061-2432
609-555-9783

Objective: A position as Manager of Technical Services with Indiana University Library.

QUALIFICATIONS

- Supervisory and administrative experience in a highly automated library environment.
- State-of-the-art knowledge of serial automation.
- Strong background in acquisitions, cataloging, and processing.
- Experience in a university environment.

WORK EXPERIENCE

Head, Cataloging and Systems Department, 1991–present
Swarthmore College Library, Swarthmore, PA

- Administer all cataloging and systems activities of the library and supervise 15 staff members in this department.
- Utilize MARC, DDC, AACR2, OCLC, LC subject headings, and authority control.
- Coordinate use of NOTIS and all library network activities.
- Streamlined cataloging operation, which reduced processing time by one week.
- Serve as liaison to the Pennsylvania Consortium of College Libraries.

Product and Customer Service Manager, 1988–91
Layman Library Services, Harrisonburg, VA

- Planned and designed serials and acquisitions components of integrated library automation system.
- Coordinated user group newsletter and forums at national conferences.
- Demonstrated systems to libraries on a routine basis.
- Honored with "Product Manager of the Year" award for consistently high performance.

Head of Serials, 1985–88
University of Chicago, Graduate Library, Chicago, IL

- Supervised all serials activities including cataloging, claiming, check-in, binding, and replacement.
- Oversaw ongoing reclassification.
- Planned and implemented transition to automated serials system.
- Headed updating of University of Chicago Library Consortium Union List of Serials.

Serials Cataloger, 1983–85
Florida Southern College, Lakeland, FL 33102

- Performed and revised all serials cataloging.
- Established and maintained series authority file.
- Processed continuations and checked in nonperiodical series using OCLC serials control subsystem.
- Cataloged microfilms, music scores, and monographs in areas of music and literature.

EDUCATION

M.L.S., Kent State University, Kent, Ohio, 1983.

M.A., History, Fordham University, New York, NY, 1981.

B.A., English Literature, Hamilton College, Clinton, NY, 1979.

PROFESSIONAL MEMBERSHIP AND ACTIVITIES

American Library Association

Association for Library Collections and Technical Services
- Chair, Serials Section Committee to Study Serials Standards, 1993–94.
- Chair, Serials Section Union Lists of Serials Committee, 1990–91.

Association of College and Research Libraries
- Standards and Accreditation Committee, 1992–93.
- Academic Status Committee, 1989–90.

Pennsylvania Library Association
- Chair, Library Technology Subgroup, 1994–95. Planned and implemented a major program on networking at the 1995 annual conference.

North American Serials Interest Group
- Electronic Communications Committee, 1993–94.

PRESENTATIONS

- Workshop Presenter, "Union Lists: A Sheep in Wolf's Clothing?" at North American Serials Interest Group, 1995.

- ACRL Mid-Atlantic Serials Group presentation, "Standards That Will Change Your World," September 1995.

- Presenter, Computers in Libraries Conference, "Acquisitions: Don't Look Back!", June 1994.

Figure 7.4. Sample Resume—Elizabeth Keller

ELIZABETH B. KELLER

2144 California St. #611 • Ithaca, NY 14853 • Office: 803-555-6546
Home: 803-555-6425 • E-mail: ebkeller@aol.com

Objective: To serve as Media Services Director, Montgomery County Schools, Rockville, MD.

Educational Philosophy

Students deserve the opportunities to use their unique talents and abilities in their quest for learning. The library media program provides materials, instruction, and curriculum integration to maximize learning situations to meet the needs of staff and students. Lifelong learners become literate, contributing members of society.

Qualifications

- Broad-based experience in all areas of media coordination and development.
- Extensive automation skills, including online circulation/cataloging and networking.
- Strong interpersonal skills in working with students, teachers, and parents.
- Successful manager of Instructional Media Center.

Experience

District Media Coordinator and Instructional Media Center Director, Ithaca Area School District, Ithaca, NY, 1990–present.

- Coordinated automation of circulation and cataloging in all district Instructional Media Centers.
- Revised and implemented board policies for copyright selection/reconsideration and community use of facilities.
- Obtained funding for retrospective conversion and CD-ROM database materials—one of 12 in the state.
- Developed Long Range Media Strategic Plan.
- Revised K–12 Scope and Sequence for Library Media Skills.
- Opened new John Adams Elementary School with Novell networked computers throughout the building and served as building system's administrator.
- Led Tactic Team to plan student assessment and achievement.

Ithaca Summer EXCEL Director, Summers 1992–94.

- Planned and directed the summer school program, grades pre–K through 12.
- Devised budget, hired 4 staff members, and coordinated course offerings and support services.
- Supervised daily operation of the program.

Elizabeth B. Keller, Page 2

Library Media Specialist (K–5 and 6–8 grades), Highland County Schools, Monterey, VA., 1982–90.

- Developed training program for computers and new library research skills curriculum.
- Acquired funding for materials through *Staunton News Leader* grants, book fairs, and private donations.
- Reallocated elementary library space—created a story corner with puppet theater and computer lab.
- Managed computer hardware/software use including maintenance and purchases.
- Developed library skills curriculum and literature appreciation activities.
- Coordinated first system telelecture.
- Initiated VCR use in elementary school.
- Implemented reading enrichment programs through book clubs and annual read-in/sleep-over activities.
- Opened new middle school library with automated catalog and circulation.

Additional Work Experience

1981–82	Document Specialist	Advanced Computers, Inc., Waynesboro, VA.
1977–81	Reference Librarian	Mary Baldwin College, Staunton, VA.
1976–77	Graduate Assistant	Clark Atlanta University, Atlanta, GA.
1974–76	English Teacher	Atlanta Public School System, Atlanta, GA.

Education

Master of Science in Library Science, Clark Atlanta University, School of Library and Information Science, Atlanta, GA, 1977.

Bachelor of Science in Chemistry, Morehouse College, Atlanta, GA, 1974.

Certificates and Licenses

- Educational Administration Certification Program, New York University, New York.
- Permanent Professional Certificate, State of Georgia: English 7–12 and Library Media Specialist/Librarian.
- 5-year Professional License, State of New York: Library Media Supervisor, English Teacher 7–12.

Honors and Awards

- Chrysler Family Reading Grant Recipient, 1994.
- Finalist for American Association of School Librarians, National School Library Media Program of the Year Award, 1993.
- *Staunton News Leader* Educators Grant Recipient: 1983, 1985, 1987.
- 3M/JMRT (Junior Members Round Table, American Library Association) Professional Grant Recipient, 1979.

Professional Association Activities ═══════════════════════════════

American Library Association
- Councilor, elected at-large, 1990–93.
- Council Caucus Chair, 1992–93. Led meeting of council members to review issues.
- Junior Members Round Table
    Chair, Olofson Grant Committee, 1981.
    Chair, Committee on Governance, 1984–85.
    Director of Publications, 1985–86.
- American Association of School Librarians
    Chair, Microcomputers in the Schools Award Committee, 1987.
    Member, Long-Range Planning Committee.
- Library Administration and Management Association
    Member, Staff Development Committee, 1991–93.
- New York Educational Media Association
    Member, Awards Committee, 1990–92.
    School Restructuring Ad-Hoc Committee, 1993.

Publications ═══

- Regular columnist for *Library Talk*, 1988–90.
- "A Library Skills Curriculum for Elementary School Students," *Library Talk*, April 1990.
- Co-editor for new journal in development—*HITS: Helping Integrate Topics in Schools.*

Community Involvement ══

- Highland County Cable Commission, 1987–90.
- Ithaca Public Library Board, 1995–present.
- Girl Scout Leader, 1993–present.

Figure 7.5. Sample Curriculum Vitae—Constance MacPherson

CURRICULUM VITAE

CONSTANCE A. MACPHERSON

Clarion University of Pennsylvania
College of Communication, Computer Information Science and Library Science
109 Becker Hall
Clarion, PA 16214
814-555-6638 FAX: 814-555-4311
E-mail: macph@aol.com

OBJECTIVE: Dean of a school of library and information science.

HIGHLIGHTS OF QUALIFICATIONS

- Ten years of teaching experience at university level.
- Ph.D. in library and information studies.
- Recognized authority on school library media programs.
- Author of numerous articles on all aspects of librarianship.

EDUCATION

Drexel University	Ph.D.	Library and Information Studies, 1992
University of Pittsburgh	M.S.	Computer Education and Cognitive Systems, 1992
University of Pittsburgh	M.L.S.	Specialization: School Libraries, 1974
Sarah Lawrence College	B.A.	English and Education, 1973

WORK EXPERIENCE

Assistant Professor, School Library Media Program, 1993 to present.
Clarion University of Pennsylvania, College of Communication, Computer Information Science and Library Science, Clarion, PA.

- Taught children's services and literature, computer applications for libraries, information technologies, and school libraries.
- Extensive research in the following areas:
  Innovation diffusion and technology integration in school library media centers and graduate library education.
  Impact of school library media centers on academic achievement.
  Communication channels of school library media specialists.

School of Library and Information Science, University of Pittsburgh, Pittsburgh, PA.

Adjunct Professor/Doctoral Research Associate, 1991–92.
- Taught courses in children's and young adult literature.
- Provided online and research services for the faculty of the University's Pennsylvania Center for Educational Technology (PCET).
- Taught bibliographic instruction for PCET workshops and classes.

Director, Information Retrieval Laboratory/Doctoral Teaching Associate, 1989–92.
- Taught courses in media production and services, local area networks, computers for libraries, and children's literature.
- Supervised all laboratory operations and Master's level student lab assistants.
- Conducted bibliographic instruction and class demonstrations of CD-ROM databases, including OCLC.

ADDITIONAL WORK HISTORY

1985–89	Elementary Library Media Specialist, King George County Schools, Bronxville, NY.
1984–85	High School Librarian, Troy County Public Schools, Troy, NY.
1983	Government Documents/Reference Librarian, Long Island Library District, Montauk, NY.
1976–78	Elementary Librarian, Fairfield School District, Greenwich, CT.

CURRENT RESEARCH

"The Impact of School Library Media Centers in Pennsylvania on Academic Achievement." Sponsored by the School Library Media Section of the New York Library Association, 1994–96, $5,000.

"The School Library Media Specialist: A Proposed Model." Research in progress.

"Children and Youth Service in Library Education." Coauthored with Chantelle Miller; research in progress.

ARTICLES

"Electronic Resources in ALA Accredited Library Schools." Recently submitted to *Library Journal.*

"Attitudes of School Library Media Specialists Toward Networking," *School Library Media Quarterly*, Summer 1995.

"Credentialing of Online Database Searchers," coauthored with Ralph Brite, *LIBRES: Library and Information Science Research Electronic Journal,* No. 3, October 1992.

Frequent contributor and book/software reviewer to:
- *School Library Journal*
- *Emergency Librarian*
- *Library Journal*

Children's book reviewer/previewer for Harcourt Brace, HarperCollins, and Scholastic.

Manuscript referee for *School Library Media Quarterly, School Libraries Worldwide,* and *Emergency Librarian.*

PAPER AND PROGRAM PRESENTATIONS

"Electronic Resources for School Library Media Specialists," research program presented at the Association of Library and Information Science Educators (ALISE), National Conference, Salt Lake City, UT, February 1995.

"School Library Media Centers and Impact on Academic Achievement," program presented at the American Association of School Librarians (AASL) National Conference, Cleveland, OH, October 1994.

"Recent Trends in Children's Literature," program presented to the Reading Teachers Association of Western Pennsylvania, May 1994.

"The Role of the School Library in Library Networks," paper presented at New York Library Association, Albany, NY, 1990.

Numerous workshops and institutes for school districts and local conferences, particularly on computer applications for libraries and technology integration into curriculum.

GRANTS

U. S. Department of Education, Title IIB of the Higher Education Act, Library Training for School Library Media Specialist, 1993–94. Grant for $20,000.

New York Library Association Research Grant, 1994–96. Grant for $5,500 for research on "The Impact of School Library Media Centers in Pennsylvania on Academic Achievement."

PROFESSIONAL ASSOCIATION ACTIVITIES

AMERICAN LIBRARY ASSOCIATION

    American Association of School Librarians (AASL)
        Candidate for AASL Treasurer; June 1996 election.
        Restructuring Taskforce, 1995–96.
        Research Committee, 1993–97; Chair, 1995–96.
        Highsmith Research Award Committee, 1994–95.
        Lance Study Replication Committee, 1994–96.
        Membership Committee, 1986–89; Chair, 1987–89.
        Microcomputers in the School Library Award Committee, Chair, 1990.
        School Library Media Program of the Year Award Committee, 1991.

    Association for Library Services to Children
        Boy Scouts of America Advisory Committee, 1991–93, Chair, 1992–93.

    Library Administration and Management Association
        BES-School Libraries Facility Committee, 1987–90.

    Young Adult Library Services Association
        Computer Applications Committee, 1991–94; Chair, 1993–94.

    Library Research Round Table
        Chair-Elect, 1994–95; Chair, 1995–96.
        Executive Board, Member-at-Large, 1993–96.

INTERNATIONAL ASSOCIATION OF SCHOOL LIBRARIANS
    Editorial Board, IASL Journal, *School Libraries Worldwide*, 1994–97.

PENNSYLVANIA LIBRARY ASSOCIATION
    Continuing Education Committee, 1993–95.
    School Library Media Section
        Research Committee, 1995–97; Chair, 1995.
        Executive Board, 1994–96.

HONORS AND AWARDS

- *Who's Who in America 1995.*
- Beta Phi Mu (National Library Science Honor Society), 1974.
- Phi Delta Kappa (National Education Fraternity), 1986.
- Presidential Academic Scholarship, Sarah Lawrence College, 1969.

INSTITUTIONAL AND COMMUNITY SERVICE

Clarion University of Pennsylvania
    Computing and Instructional Technology (CIT) Committee, 1994–present.
    Becker Hall Space Planning Task Force, 1994–95.
    Curriculum Committee, 1993–96; Chair, 1994–96.

Parent Teacher Student Association (PTSA) Volunteer
    Educational Policy Committee, Central School District, 1993–94.
    American Educator Awards Committee, 1994–96; Chair, 1994–96.

Certified National U. S. Swimming Stroke and Turn Official.

Figure 7.6. Sample Resume—Dean Myers

DEAN R. MYERS
2616 N. Rodeo Drive
Salt Lake City, UT 04103
Office: 612-555-2433

OBJECTIVE

Assistant Director of a public library system.

QUALIFICATIONS

- Significant supervisory and administrative experience in large public library.
- Broad experience in managing branch libraries of different sizes.
- Excellent knowledge of automated systems and new technologies.

WORK EXPERIENCE

Salt Lake City Public Library System, Salt Lake City, UT.

Branch Manager, Pinedale Branch, 1992–present
- Managed largest branch in library system (annual circulation exceeding one million).
- Proposed, designed, and implemented Division for the Visually Handicapped.
- Served as chair of Public Library System Staff Development Committee.
- Supervised an ethnically diverse staff of 30 employees.
- Coordinated move and opening of 26,000 square foot branch library.

Branch Manager, Galleria Mall Branch, 1989–92

- Managed busy storefront branch in shopping mall.
- Designed and implemented library computer center.
- Applied for and received grant to have a mural painted in the library as part of the Art for Public Places Program.
- Coordinated a program for latchkey children that was nationally recognized in library press.
- Led book discussion groups on a monthly basis.

Head, Youth Services Department, Central Library, 1987–89

- Planned, directed, and implemented all library services for children.
- Supervised staff of 7.
- Implemented a wide range of electronic resources for children.
- Designed outreach activities including local school visits.
- Gained excellent knowledge of children's literature.

EDUCATION

M.L.S., University of Maryland, College of Library and Information Science, 1985.

B.A., Political Science, Lynchburg College, Lynchburg, VA, 1982.

**PROFESSIONAL
ACTIVITIES**

Maryland Library Association
- Elected to several leadership positions including: President, 1993–94, and Treasurer, 1992–93
- Chair, Reference Interest Group

American Library Association
   Young Adult Library Services Association
- Chair, YALSA Intellectual Freedom Committee

Represented Maryland Library Association at ALA/Intellectual Freedom Committee Leadership Training Institute.

Figure 7.7. Sample Resume—Sally Walter

SALLY T. WALTER
Emporia State University Libraries
P.O. Box 402
Emporia, KS 66801
316-555-5203

Objective: To serve as a Director or Head of Public Services for a university.

SUMMARY OF QUALIFICATIONS

- Experience in all aspects of public services in a university setting.
- Implemented new policies and procedures which improved customer service.
- Supervised staff in public services and security.
- Extensive background in interlibrary loan.

WORK EXPERIENCE

**Access Services Department Head (1989–present) and
Assistant Professor of Bibliography (1992–present),
Emporia State University Libraries, Emporia, KS.**

Management and Administration
- Supervised, trained, and evaluated 8 Access Services staff.
- Administered department budget and submit yearly plan.
- Managed all building security.
- Collected and analyzed a wide range of data for management and strategic planning.

Circulation
- Formulated and implemented a proposal for telephone notification of overdue materials.
- Created a Reserve customer satisfaction survey.
- Implemented a borrower's card policy that has resulted in income of over $6,000 to date.
- Trained personnel on circulation functions of NOTIS.
- Created a customer service satisfaction survey analysis for interlibrary loan.

Teaching
- Teach one course every semester. Courses include Staff Development in Libraries; Introduction to Bibliography; and History of the Book.

ADDITIONAL WORK EXPERIENCE

Government Documents Librarian, University of Puerto Rico, San Juan, PR, 1988–89.

Media Librarian, College of Eduction, Learning Resource Center, Yale University, New Haven, CT, 1987–88.

EDUCATION

M.L.S., Emporia State University, Emporia, KS, 1987.

B.S., Education Technology, Tufts University, Medford, MA, 1985.

PRESENTATIONS/WORKSHOPS

"Emporia State University Gopher Menu," School of Library and Information Management, Emporia State University, January 1996.

"Accommodating Change Through Training," Association of College and Research Libraries Conference, Salt Lake City, UT, April 1995.

"Training for Automated Circulation Systems," panel presenter, Annual Conference, Kansas Library Association, 1995.

PUBLICATIONS

"The Future of Access Services," with Jane Terra, *Collection Management*, Jan. 1996, vol. 5, p. 12.

"Circulation Desk Operations," *College and Research Libraries News* 52, p. 994.

PROFESSIONAL ACTIVITIES

Kansas Library Association
  • Automation Round Table, Chair, 1993–94.
  • Interlibrary Loan Cooperation Committee, 1994–95.

American Library Association
    Association of College and Research Libraries
      • Chapters Council, 1995.
    Library Administration and Management Association
      • Staff Development Committee—Coordinated major revision of *Staff Development: A Practical Guide.*

AWARDS

Emporia State University Associates Distinguished Lectureship, 1994.

Emporia State University Faculty Career Development Award, 1995.

3 LIBRARY SCHOOL STUDENT (RECENT GRADUATE)— SAMPLE RESUMES

Writing a resume can be especially challenging for those just graduating from library school or just beginning their careers. In this chapter, we will examine resumes of individuals who have virtually no professional experience as well as those who have had one position after graduation. Here are some pointers to assist you in this process:

1. When you don't have significant work experience, a functional format will usually serve you best.
2. Think carefully about professional and volunteer experiences. Be sure to indicate any leadership positions. Don't forget that employers are looking for potential.
3. Identify any courses you have completed in graduate school that are germane to the position. Emphasize an M.L.S. degree by including it under the qualifications heading.
4. Don't be afraid to mention nonprofessional work experience. There are some skills in these positions that are transferable to professional positions.
5. Be sure to include skills and accomplishments from other nonlibrary professional positions. Oral and written communication abilities can be particularly relevant.

Now let's get to know some recent graduates.

Madeline Andrus is applying for a position as Librarian I/Bibliographer for the social sciences and journalism. The job posting stresses the following areas as being critical: subject expertise in journalism and social sciences, knowledge of a foreign language, and good oral and written communication skills. Madeline's resume reflects the excellent job she did completing her personal inventory—she references a number of useful professional and outside activities that support her qualifications for this position (see Figure 8.1).

Irene Bennett completed her M.L.S. about a year ago and has had several good temporary positions. Her goal is a permanent position as a reference librarian, and Irene is applying for a specific job in an academic library. At first glance, it might appear that a functional format would be most advantageous for Irene. In this case, however, she uses the chronological format because virtually all of Irene's experience is in reference and applies directly to the position (see Figure 8.2). Note that Irene includes a position where she did intensive telephone work; while not in a library, it certainly demonstrates her flexibility and ability to deal with pressure.

Max Franklin is applying for a position as a children's librarian in a large public library. Although he doesn't have a great deal of experience, he has documented significant activities related to service to children. He has used a functional format to create a very effective one-page resume (see Figure 8.3).

Walter James seeks a business reference librarian position in a university. Note how effectively he uses the one-liners to support his job objective (see Figure 8.4). Also, his choice of the functional format helps showcase his most relevant skill area.

Rachel Smith is a recent library school graduate who has just completed a one-year position as a librarian with a government advisory commission that is going out of business. While her job search is focused on association and nonprofit organization libraries, she is also interested in newspaper libraries that might capitalize on her previous experience as a reporter. Since her professional library experience is somewhat limited, Rachel chooses a functional format for her resume to highlight the good range of skills she has acquired in library as well as nonlibrary positions (see Figure 8.5). Because she anticipates that her prospective employer may not have a library background, she has paid special attention to describing her experience in clear terms. Although she lacks professional association involvement, she has not forgotten relevant volunteer work.

Figure 8.1. Sample Resume—Madeline Andrus

MADELINE C. ANDRUS
311 W. Chestnut Street
Milwaukee, WI 53222
Home: 414-555-4313

Objective: Librarian I/Bibliographer for the Social Sciences and Journalism at the University of California, Los Angeles.

QUALIFICATIONS

- Master of Library and Information Science with course work in collection development.
- Subject expertise in journalism and social sciences.
- Experience working in an academic environment.
- Solid writing skills.

EXPERIENCE

COLLECTION DEVELOPMENT
- Undergraduate journalism degree with additional course work in economics, sociology, and government.
- Completed graduate course in collection development.
- Working knowledge of German.
- As reference intern in college library, served students at reference desk.

ORAL COMMUNICATION
- As reference intern, extensive interaction with students in college library.
- Regularly participated in German-language discussion group.
- Spoke with wide range of clients as courseware developer.

WRITTEN COMMUNICATION
- Wrote and administered an evaluation of College Library Skills Instruction Program.
- Prepared summary report on evaluation.
- Wrote thesis entitled: *Collection Development in Women's History*.
- As courseware developer, wrote extensive documentation.

WORK HISTORY

Reference Intern, College Library, University of Wisconsin-Milwaukee, WI, 1995.

Courseware Developer, Walcott-Taylor Company, Inc., Milwaukee, WI, 1993–95.

EDUCATION

M.L.I.S., University of Wisconsin-Milwaukee, WI, 1996.

B.A., Journalism, University of Wisconsin-Madison, WI, 1993. Graduated cum laude.

PUBLICATIONS

- Assisted with research and bibliography for *Networking and Resources Sharing: Case Studies*, by Roger Bassett. Neal-Schuman Publishers 1998.

PROFESSIONAL ACTIVITIES

ALA Student Chapter
- Student Orientation Committee, 1995. Proposed to faculty that student association assist in the planning and implementation of fall orientation for new library school students. Served as chair of first committee.

Member: American Library Association, Special Libraries Association.

OTHER ACTIVITIES

- German Round Table—Regular participant in activities related to German-language studies.
- Enjoy Middle Eastern cooking, reading German literature, and listening to opera.

Figure 8.2. Sample Resume—Irene Bennett

Irene E. Bennett

854 W. Broad Street
Pittsburgh, PA 15213-3890
Home: 812-555-3219 Office: 812-555-5234
E-mail: ibenn@aol.com

Objective: To work as a reference librarian at Hunt Library Information Center, Carnegie-Mellon University.

Qualifications
- Excellent reference skills
- Experience working with undergraduate students
- Broad range of database searching including Internet
- Strong interpersonal skills

Work Experience

University of Pittsburgh, Undergraduate Library

Temporary Reference Librarian, 1995–96
- Provided in-person reference service to undergraduate students.
- Experience with numerous computer platforms including Mac, DOS, Windows, and UNIX.
- Extensive database experience including NEXIS, DIALOG, and the World Wide Web.
- Assisted in the development of user surveys to assess the quality of bibliographic instruction.
- Evaluated CD-ROM products on a regular basis.

Bibliographic Instruction Assistant, 1995
- Instructed groups of students on how to use a wide range of library sources (both print and electronic).
- Developed tip sheet on using CD-ROM sources.
- Compiled results of class evaluations.
- Provided in-person service to students using online sources.

The University of Alabama, Hurt Memorial Library, Tuscaloosa, AL

Reference Assistant, 1994–95
- Provided in-person and telephone reference assistance.
- Assisted professors with establishing reserve collections for class reference.
- Instructed students on use of Internet sources.

Instruction Assistant, 1994
- Gave tours of library facilities.
- Assisted in student workshops on electronic sources.

Royal Business Suites, Fremont, AL
  Administrative Assistant, 1993–94
- Answered telephone and took reservations for executive business suites company.
- Assisted up to 40 clients on an hourly basis.
- Received "Customer Service Excellence Award" for outstanding service.

Consulting Experience
- Prepared bibliography for inclusion in *The Single Mother* and *The Single Mother Sourcebook*, by Paula James, Apprentice Press, Pittsburgh, PA, 1994.
- Searched library and information science literature and prepared bibliography about evaluation of school library programs. For research conducted by Helen Eames, Associate Dean for Academic Studies, 1994.

Education

Master of Library Science, The University of Alabama, School of Library and Information Studies, Tuscaloosa, AL, 1994.

Bachelor of Arts, German and History, Chatham College, Pittsburgh, PA, 1992.

Volunteer Experience

- Research Paper Clinic Volunteer, Undergraduate Library Services, University of Pittsburgh. Provided in-depth assistance to students during half-hour sessions on selection of appropriate sources and instruction in the use of those sources, 1995.

- Student Mentor Program, Tuscaloosa, AL. Worked with high school students with learning disabilities, 1994.

Professional Activities

- Member, American Library Association.

Figure 8.3. Sample Resume—Max Franklin

Max W. Franklin

16 W. Memorial Parkway, Atglen, PA 19102 • 602-555-1524 • Mfranklin@aol.com

Objective: To work as Children's Librarian for Westchester County Public Library.

Qualifications
- M.L.S. with significant course work in children's literature and library service to youth.
- Experience in working with children in a public library.
- Volunteer reader to children.
- Experienced with PCs and databases.

Experience

Service to Children
- Graduate coursework in children's literature.
- Current experience working with children in New York Public Library.
- Wrote thesis entitled *Kindergarten Library Program Enrichment.*
- Read in Saturday Story Hour for children.

Automation Skills
- Completed several graduate courses related to automation.
- Searching experience using a wide range of databases.
- Completed independent study project on children's resources on the Internet.
- Worked with microcomputers and networked system.

Job History
- Library clerk (part-time), New York Public Library, New York, 1994–95.
- Administrative assistant, Swinehart and Associates, New York, NY, 1992–93.

Education
- Master of Library Science, Syracuse University, Syracuse, NY, 1996.
- B.A., English, Oberlin College, Oberlin, OH, 1994.

Professional Involvement

New York Library Association
- Children and Young Adult Interest Group, 1995–96. Active participant on Annual Conference Program Subcommittee—assisted in the planning of 1996 program on "Diversity in Children's Literature."

New York Literacy Council
- Newsletter, 1995. Assisted in the production and distribution of this publication.

Volunteer Story Reader, Brooklyn Public Library, 1994–95.
- Regularly participated in Saturday Children's Story Hour.

Other Activities
- Swimmer, antique collector, and cross-country skier.

Figure 8.4. Sample Resume—Walter James

Walter L. James
23 Hamilton Drive
Bronx, NY 11225
Office: 718-555-2305 Home: 718-555-6231
E-mail: wjames@aol.com

Objective: Business Reference Librarian, University of Oregon Library.

QUALIFICATIONS

- M.L.S. graduate with specialization in reference.
- Excellent background in business reference.
- Wide range of database skills.
- B.A. in business administration.
- Outstanding writing and speaking abilities.

EXPERIENCE

Reference

- Provided reference assistance in fast-paced Wall Street firm.
- Excellent knowledge of wide range of business reference sources.
- Completed coursework in business reference sources in library school.

Database Searching/Automation

- Experienced searcher in many business databases.
- Good knowledge of microcomputers.
- Working knowledge of a wide range of software packages.
- Expert Internet searcher.

Writing and Speaking

- Awarded prize for outstanding thesis.
- Experienced speaker at professional library association meetings.
- Assisted library school professor in the writing of *Business Reference Sources for Everyone*.

JOB HISTORY

Library Clerk (part-time), Harrison Forecasters, New York, NY, 1995–96.

Pizza deliverer, Tony's Pizzeria, Bronx, New York, 1995.

Sales Associate, Tiffany & Company, New York, NY, 1994.

EDUCATION

Master of Library Science, Rutgers University, New Brunswick, NJ, 1995.

Bachelor of Arts in Business Administration, Long Island University, Brookville, NY, 1993.

PROFESSIONAL ACTIVITIES

New York Library Association
- Member, Business Round Table, 1996. Coordinated and led program on "Business Reference Sources on the Internet."
- Treasurer, Legislative Day.

American Library Association
- Member: New Members Round Table and Library and Information Technology Association.

OTHER ACTIVITIES

- Reader, New York Tapes for the Blind. Read books and newspapers that are taped for the blind.
- Bird watcher, hiker, and skier.

Figure 8.5. Sample Resume—Rachel Smith	

RACHEL R. SMITH
1220 Belvedere Lane
Chevy Chase, MD 20895
(301) 555-1270

OBJECTIVE	Librarian with an association or nonprofit organization
QUALIFICATIONS	Expert searching skills using a wide range of databases Reference experience with scientific and technical emphasis Ability to work well in high pressure environment Experienced Internet searcher Extensive writing and interviewing experience
EXPERIENCE	**Database and Internet Searching** • Extensive searching experience using Dialog, LEXIS/NEXIS, MEDLARS, and OCLC. Special emphasis on scientific and medical searching. • Internet searching including the use of telnet, gophers, Mosaic, and Netscape. • Maintained publications database using Lotus Notes. **Reference and Bibliography** • As sole librarian for the Advisory Commission on Child Nutrition, provided extensive reference service to nutritionists, doctors, and other researchers for scientific and technical information. • Created bibliographies using a variety of online databases. • Initiated interlibrary loans with other government agencies. • Conducted in-depth telephone reference interviews with Maryland state legislative staff. **Library Support Services** • Weeded and conducted inventory of a technical library. • Member of a team that moved a library to another location. **Writing and Media Relations** • For Member of Congress, wrote press releases and maintained media contacts. • Responded to press inquiries and arranged interviews. • Wrote articles for and designed newsletters. • As newspaper reporter for *The Daily Progress* and *Town Crier*, wrote news and feature articles.
WORK HISTORY	1994–present Librarian, Advisory Commission on Child Nutrition 1994 Intern Technical Library, Wisconsin Comptroller of Public Accounts 1991–93 Information Specialist, Maryland State Legislative Reference Service, Telephone Inquiry Unit 1987–91 Press Assistant and Computer Operator/Press Secretary for Senator Josephine S. Teller 1986–87 Reporter, *The Daily Progress*, Asheville, NC 1984–86 Reporter, *Town Crier*, Bishop, TN

Rachel Smith, Page 2

EDUCATION

Master of Arts, School of Library and Information Studies, University of Wisconsin-Madison, Madison, Wisconsin, 1994.

Bachelor of Science in Mass Communications, East Tennessee State University, Johnson City, TN, 1984. Minor in political science. Cum laude.

VOLUNTEER WORK

1993, Montgomery County Public Library, Silver Spring Branch
- Shelved books and read shelves. Assisted patrons.

1991, National Endowment for the Arts, Washington, DC
- Conducted searches using NWA library database.
- Provided information and referrals for grant applicants.
- Researched and responded to written requests for information.

PROFESSIONAL ORGANIZATIONS

Member, Special Libraries Association and American Library Association

9 SPECIAL LIBRARIAN— SAMPLE RESUMES

This chapter examines resumes used to apply for positions in a wide range of libraries—corporate, law, foundation, government, and association. Here are some tips to keep in mind:

1. Be especially wary of using library jargon and acronyms. Remember that the hiring official in a law firm or association may not recognize the significance of information that would be readily apparent to someone with a library background. Take care to explain your position in straightforward language.
2. When applying for corporate positions, pay particular attention to quantifying your accomplishments. Remember that companies are bottom-line and results oriented.

Our samples are from the following group.

Sarah Hickman has worked in one position as the only librarian with a small association. She now seeks a better position as a trainer with a database company. Having chosen a functional format, note how well Sarah incorporates skills she has acquired in professional activities and outside interests (see Figure 9.1).

Albert Johnson has a real challenge: he is seeking a supervisory position, but lacks extensive work-related experience in this area. However, he has demonstrated leadership experience in professional and outside activities, so he has chosen the functional format to highlight this experience (see Figure 9.2).

Roberta Lieberman has acquired an impressive work history related to special collections cataloging. She chooses the chronological format to highlight the prestigious institutions for which she has worked (see Figure 9.3). Note how effectively she has documented professional memberships and activities, publications, presentations, and exhibitions.

Sheila Marie O'Connor has had two jobs after library school and is applying for a position as assistant head in a large scientific library. Note that she accounts for periods of unemployment (see Figure 9.4). The chronological format effectively showcases her relevant experience.

Lisa Randolph is a law librarian with the federal government and seeks a senior position in a private law firm. She carefully considered both the functional and chronological formats, but decided on the chronological since she wanted to highlight her current job with the U.S. Court of Appeals (see Figure 9.5).

Elaine Todd has lost her job because the nonprofit organization she works for has gone through a major downsizing. She is applying for a position in an association library that does a significant amount of business reference and has good skills that would be useful in this setting. Because several of her most recent positions have been with education-related groups, Elaine thinks the functional format will highlight her accomplishments better than a chronological one (see Figure 9.6).

Kyle Valente is seeking a position as director of a law library with a private firm. He chooses the chronological format since he can demonstrate good career progression that directly relates to this target position (see Figure 9.7).

Leigh Whitney-Jenkins is a client representative with a well-known library vendor. She is now applying for a marketing and events coordinator position with another vendor. Notice her emphasis on demonstrating her background in customer service, a key component of her desired position (see Figure 9.8). The chronological format is effective in demonstrating her career progression.

Figure 9.1. Sample Resume—Sarah Hickman

SARAH R. HICKMAN

National Snack Food Association, 1700 N. Conway Ave., Reston, VA 22090
Office: 703-555-4151 E-mail: srhickman@aol.com

OBJECTIVE

To work as trainer for LEXIS/NEXIS.

QUALIFICATIONS

- Skilled in training and developing training programs.
- Knowledge of a wide range of databases.
- Excellent writing and communication skills.
- Able to manage multiple demands in deadline-oriented environment.
- Master of Science in Library and Information Science.

ACCOMPLISHMENTS

Training

- Developed a training program for users of SearchMagic databases in a networked environment.
- Trained volunteers to be adult literacy tutors.
- Taught basic reading skills to adults.

Automation

- Developed library databases, including a book catalog, using DB/Textworks software.
- Redesigned InMagic reports and databases to better meet user needs.
- Designed and implemented an Internet Gopher.
- Maintained electronic book and serials catalog.

Communication Skills

- Wrote abstracts for biweekly association publication.
- Developed materials to promote member services.
- Led committee on intellectual freedom for local library association.
- Edited the newsletter of the Washington Literacy Council.

WORK HISTORY

Senior Information Specialist, National Snack Food Association, 1995–present.

Senior Sales Associate, Crate and Barrel, 1993–94.

EDUCATION

Master of Science in Library and Information Science, Pratt Institute, Brooklyn, NY, 1993.

Bachelor of Arts, Computer Science, Johns Hopkins University, Baltimore, MD, 1991.

PROFESSIONAL ACTIVITIES

- Chair, Intellectual Freedom Committee, District of Columbia Library Association. Coordinated major program for Banned Book Week.
- Washington Literacy Center: Certified Tutor, 1994; Certified Trainer, 1995.
- Member, Special Libraries Association.

Figure 9.2. Sample Resume—Albert Johnson

Albert R. Johnson

Library of the Virginia House of Delegates
1 Courthouse Square
Richmond, VA 22302
804-555-2121

Objective: Position as Supervisory Librarian in the Virginia State Library.

Qualifications

- Demonstrated leadership skills in a wide range of positions.
- Extensive reference and automation background.
- Outstanding interpersonal skills.
- Committed to providing the best client service possible.

Skills and Accomplishments

Leadership and Supervision

- Served as Acting Supervisor of Library of Virginia House of Delegates Library for four months. Supervised 8 employees.
- Led committee to choose vendor for network.
- Coordinated all conference programs for the Virginia Library Association.
- Chaired team that visited each member of the House of Delegates to solicit information needs.
- Served as President of alumni association.

Reference

- Provided telephone and in-person reference to members and staff of House of Delegates.
- Searched NEXIS/LEXIS, DIALOG, Westlaw, Datatimes, Internet, and CD-ROM products.
- Assisted with collection development of the "hotline collection."
- Specialized in searching sources related to business in Virginia.

Work Summary

Information Research Specialist, Library of the Virginia House of Delegates, Richmond, VA, 1985–present.

Research Analyst, Virginia Department of Commerce, Richmond, VA, 1983–85.

Library Technician, University of Richmond Library, Richmond, VA, 1982.

Education

M.L.S., Catholic University of America, Washington, DC, 1981.
B.A., Business Administration, University of Rhode Island, Kingston, RI, 1980.

Professional Activities

Special Libraries Association
- Chair, Government Relations Committee, 1992–94.

Virginia Library Association
- Member, Library Legislative Day Committee, 1991–93.

President, The Catholic University of America, School of Library and Information Science Alumni Board, 1994–95.

Figure 9.3. Sample Resume—Roberta Lieberman

ROBERTA N. LIEBERMAN
The Astor Center for History of Art
16 Franklin Avenue
Tarrytown, NY 15943
919-555-1555

OBJECTIVE: Director of a university archives or special collections.

QUALIFICATIONS

- Extensive experience in archival processing and cataloging.
- Broad knowledge of automation applications for special collections cataloging.
- Supervised a large staff of catalogers.
- Nationally recognized for work related to special collections management.

PROFESSIONAL EXPERIENCE

**Head of Collections Cataloging, The Astor Center for the History of Art,
Tarrytown, NY, 1992–present.**

- Managed archival cataloging and processing of manuscripts, photographs, and archives.
- Supervised 17 subject specialists.
- Extensive automation and database knowledge including Cuadra Star and RLIN.
- Served on project coordination team to select an integrated library system.

**Special Collections Librarian, Manton Department of Special Collections,
Main Library, San Jose State University, San Jose, CA, 1990–92.**

- Provided reference service for collection including a photo study collection of over 2 million items.
- Supervised Title II-C and California State Library Cataloging Grants.
- Specialized in Hispanic collections, including the North Collection on the Spanish Civil War and the Baja California Collection.
- Served as automation liaison with library.
- Coordinated INNOPAC implementation for special collections.

**Consultant (6-month project) to The Astor Center for the History of Art,
Tarrytown, NY, 1991–92.**

- Developed a processing, cataloging, and preservation plan for the Raymond Loewy collection consisting of 2 million drawings, diagrams, posters, and books.
- Developed and implemented database identifying all Loewy design projects.

Cataloger, Photographs Division, National Gallery of Art, Washington, DC, 1990–92.

- Cataloged master photographs for internationally known collection.
- Supervised archival processing and microfilming projects.
- Assisted in revision of National Gallery of Art Thesaurus for Graphic Materials.

Bibliographer II, Hispanic American Periodicals Index, San Jose State University, San Jose, CA, 1991.

- Indexed Spanish, Portuguese, French and English language journal articles relating to Latin American history, politics, and culture.
- Revised thesaurus and completed substantial name authority work.

EDUCATION

Master of Library Science, San Jose State University, School of Library and Information Science, San Jose, CA, 1989.

- Specialization in cataloging and classification, including advanced courses in cataloging theory and practice, subject analysis, nonprint cataloging, and acquisitions.

Graduate coursework in Latin American Studies, San Jose State University, 1987–88.

Intensive Portuguese Institute, University of California, Los Angeles, Summer 1985.

A.B. in Spanish, San Jose State University, San Jose, CA, 1986.

- Included studies in Spain (Univ. Complutense, Madrid).

LANGUAGES

Fluent in Spanish and Portuguese. Reading and writing knowledge of French and Italian.

PROFESSIONAL MEMBERSHIPS AND ACTIVITIES

Society of American Archivists

- Member, Nominating Committee, 1994.
- Mentor Program Volunteer, 1992.
- Publications Board, 1993–present.
- Member, Committee on Archival Information Exchange, 1989–92.

American Library Association
   Association of College and Research Libraries, Rare Books and Manuscripts Section
- Chair, 1993–94
- Executive Committee, 1991–92.
- Preconference Program Planning Committee, 1990–91.

   Librarians' Association of the University of California
- Professional Development Committee, 1995–97.
- Statewide Research Committee, 1986–88.

Member: Art Librarians' Society of North America, Visual Resources Association, and Online Audiovisual Catalogers.

PUBLICATIONS

"Description for Digitized Photo Archives." Published in *Image Access Project: Proceedings from an RLG Forum*, held in Monterey, CA. Mountain View, CA: Research Libraries Group, 1994.

"Cataloging Archival Photograph Collections," *Visual Resources*, v. 11 (1992), pp. 85–100.

"Rare Book Catalogers and Technology," *Rare Books and Manuscripts Librarianship*, v. 7, no. 2 (1991), pp. 70–75.

"Problems in Subject Classification in Special Format Materials." Coauthored with Steve Noll. Published in *Subject Indexing in Context* by Pat Turner. Boston: Prentice-Hall, 1989.

CONFERENCE PRESENTATIONS

"The Digital Image Access Project," invited paper, Society of American Archivists, Phoenix, AZ, September 1995.

"Processing Archival Photograph Collections," invited speaker, Seminar on Images in Libraries and Museums, Portland, OR, 1995.

"Descriptive Cataloging of Rare Books," seminar chair and speaker, Rare Books and Manuscript Section Preconference, Orlando, FL, 1994.

"Guidelines for Library Special Collections," invited speaker, University of California Conference on Photographic Collection Administration, Pasadena, CA, 1993.

OTHER PROFESSIONAL ACTIVITIES

Panelist, National Endowment for the Humanities, November 1994.

Instructor, Visual Materials Cataloging course. Columbia University, Rare Book School, 1994.

Archives Consultant, American School of Victorian Studies, London, 1995.

Invited participant, Council on Library Resources, symposium on form and genre terminology for thesauri, New Haven, CT, 1993.

EXHIBITIONS

"Images of Spain from the Manton Department of Special Collections," Main Library, 1990.

"Dreams and Design: Drawings from the Raymond Loewy Collection," The Astor Center for the History of Art, 1994. Selected, mounted, and documented exhibit.

Figure 9.4. Sample Resume—Sheila Marie O'Connor

SHEILA MARIE O'CONNOR

Pericles International Information
6412 Rockville Pike
Rockville, MD 20895
301-555-8888

OBJECTIVE: Assistant Head, Reference Section, National Agricultural Library

QUALIFICATIONS

- Highly skilled in all areas of science reference.
- Experience with a wide range of databases.
- Supervisory and administrative experience.
- Experience in managing large projects.

WORK EXPERIENCE

1994–present: Information Specialist, Pericles International Information, Rockville, MD.

- Manage an extensive online patent information network consisting of over 6 million records.
- Authored 3 user database guides which have been integrated into overall commercial user manuals.
- Design database fields and record formats.
- Supervise staff in testing prerelease versions of new systems.
- Directed all user liaison/customer support in the U.S.

1992–93: Maternity leave.

1991–92: Reference Librarian, Health Science Library, Georgetown University, Washington, DC.

- Provided comprehensive reference services in a major medical library.
- Conducted high-priority medical reference research for acute-care and emergency services on "stat" basis.
- Developed comprehensive knowledge of biomedical reference services.
- Expert knowledge of science databases including MEDLARS, DIALOG, and BRS.

EDUCATION

M.L.S., University of British Columbia, Vancouver, British Columbia, 1990.

B.A., Chemistry, Massachusetts Institute of Technology, Cambridge, MA, 1988.

PROFESSIONAL ACTIVITIES

- Member of peer review panel for the *Bulletin of the Medical Library Association*. Edited a special issue of the *Bulletin* on electronic publishing.

- Chair, Biological Sciences Group, Washington, DC chapter, Special Libraries Association, 1987.

OTHER ACTIVITIES

- Treasurer, Parkwood Community Association, 1994–95.

- Competitive swimmer.

Figure 9.5. Sample Resume—Lisa Randolph

LISA S. RANDOLPH

Library - U.S. Court of Appeals (4th Circuit)
16 Judicial Center Plaza
Denver, CO 76410
Phone: 717-555-3415

OBJECTIVE: A senior position in a private firm law library.

SUMMARY OF QUALIFICATIONS

- Supervisory experience in a law library.
- Broad knowledge of all aspects of law library operation including reference, databases, technical services, and cataloging.
- Significant budgetary and planning experience.
- Experience in providing high quality service to clients.

WORK EXPERIENCE

Librarian, Library of the U.S. Court of Appeals (4th Circuit), Denver, CO, 1991–present.

- Coordinated long-range planning for 20 branches of the Circuit library system.
- Trained library staff in cataloging and classification.
- Performed daily legal reference for staff and judges of the Court.
- Planned and administered database access and budget.

Senior Law Librarian/Head of Technical Services, Law Library, San Francisco State University, San Francisco, CA, 1990–91.

- Established and monitored cataloging and acquisition procedures.
- Supervised and trained 6 staff members.
- Administered budget for the technical services department.
- Taught LEXIS/NEXIS classes to staff and students.
- Served as Acting Director of the Law Library.

Senior Cataloger, Shared Cataloging Division, Library of Congress, Washington, DC, 1985–91.

- Performed descriptive cataloging of materials in English, French, German, and Hungarian.
- Trained new catalogers in an apprenticeship program that lasted 3 months.
- Served as a member of the Name Authority Cooperative, the national program for authority work.

EDUCATION

- Master of Science, University of Illinois at Urbana-Champaign, Graduate School of Library and Information Science, Champaign, IL, 1975.
- Bachelor of Arts, French, Princeton University, Princeton, NJ, 1972.

HONORS

- Recognition Award, U.S. Court of Appeals (4th Circuit), 1991.

- Outstanding Performance Award, Library of Congress, 1987.

PROFESSIONAL ACTIVITIES

- Faculty Member, National Conference of State Legislatures, Annual Meeting, 1992.

- Delegate, White House Conference on Library and Information Science, Washington, DC, 1979.

- Library Fellow, United States Information Agency/American Library Association, Spring 1992, Central University Library, Budapest, Hungary.

- Guest/participant, East-West Summit on Emerging Computer Technologies in Libraries, International Centre for Scientific Information, Helsinki, Finland, 1992.

- Member: American Association of Law Libraries, American Library Association, Northern California Association of Law Libraries.

Figure 9.6 Sample Resume—Elaine Todd

ELAINE S. TODD

16 Crescent Place * North Potomac, MD 20818 * (301)555-2225

OBJECTIVE

Position as an Information Specialist with the Thrift Banker's Association.

QUALIFICATIONS

- Able to work well in high-pressure environment.
- Experienced manager of association information centers.
- Excellent skills in acquisitions, cataloging, and serials control.
- Expert searcher in a wide range of databases.

EXPERIENCE

Reference Support

- Four years experience as sole information center librarian; provided wide range of reference service to public service agencies.
- Developed bibliographies on numerous topics.
- Coordinated clipping services for current awareness packets.

Automation and Database Searching

- Implemented and maintained acquisitions, cataloging, classification, and loan procedures using InMagic software.
- Developed databases for training records and mailing lists.
- Experienced searcher with LEXIS/NEXIS, Datatimes, and CD-ROM databases.
- Extensive experience searching the Internet.

Collection Development

- Selected, acquired, and processed a multimedia collection for a resource center.
- Managed a large clearinghouse of information related to education policy.
- Reviewed and annotated new titles under consideration for purchase.

WORK HISTORY	1992–94	Director	Resource Center, Child Welfare League, Bethesda, MD.
	1990–94	Manager	Information Services, Education Now Foundation, Alexandria, VA.
	1983–88	Librarian	Takoma Park Branch, Montgomery County Public Library, Takoma, MD, 1983–88.
	1983–85	Librarian	U.S. Committee for Petroleum Awareness, Washington, DC.

Elaine S. Todd   Page 2

EDUCATION

Master of Library Science, North Carolina Central University, Durham, NC, 1983.
Bachelor of Arts in Sociology, Sweet Briar College, Sweet Briar, VA, 1974. Graduated magna cum laude.

AWARDS & HONORS

- Beta Phi Mu Honor Society, 1984.
- *Who's Who Among Students in American Universities and Colleges*, 1982–83.

PROFESSIONAL ACTIVITIES

- Member, American Library Association and Special Libraries Association.
- District of Columbia Library Association
  Membership Committee, Chair, 1990–91.
  Member of Board of Directors, 1993–94.
  Chaired the Joint Spring Workshop, 1992. Coordinated one day program, "Legislative Advocacy" which was attended by over 100 librarians.

Figure 9.7. Sample Resume—Kyle Valente

Kyle R. Valente
3381 N. Eames Avenue
Kensington, MD 20895
Office: 202-555-8882 Home: 301-555-1333

Objective: Director of a library for a private law firm

Qualifications
- Extensive experience in managing all areas of a law library.
- Experience in supervising staff.
- Outstanding background in all areas of law reference.
- Known for emphasis on superior client service.

Work Experience

Head of Legislative Services; Farber, Pettavino, and Iafrate, Washington, DC, 1994–present.

- Provided reference service to 180 attorneys.
- Trained and supervised 3 legislative assistants.
- In-depth knowledge of LEXIS/NEXIS, Westlaw, DIALOG, Legi-slate, Dun and Bradstreet.
- Devised and implemented Internet training program for the entire firm, including weekly workshops and daily one-on-one training for attorneys.
- Collected and distributed all relevant legislative material.

Branch Supervisor; City of Charlotte Law Library, Charlotte, NC, 1992–94.

- Managed 18,000 volume collection.
- Provided reference service to attorney and judicial clients.
- Performed all collection development duties for the branch.
- Established policies and procedures for staff and patrons.
- Planned a move from a 3,000 square foot space to a 6,500 square foot space.
- Cited as "City Employee of the Year" for 1994 for excellence in service to the city.

Law Librarian; Hamilton, Prescott, and Mauzy, Charlotte, NC, 1990–92.

- Sole librarian for 50-attorney branch office of a large Atlanta law firm.
- Performed all legal and nonlegal reference and research using a wide range of electronic resources.
- Performed all administrative functions including collection development, budgeting, coordinating MCLE training for attorneys.
- Supervised looseleaf filing service.
- Planned and developed a new library space and implemented the move.

Education
M.L.S., University of North Carolina at Chapel Hill, Chapel Hill, SC, 1991.
M.A. in Journalism, Columbia University, New York, NY, 1989.
B.A. in Journalism, Hunter College, New York, NY, 1988.

Professional Activities
American Association of Law Librarians
- Speaker, Annual meeting in Pittsburgh, Program on "Training Reference Librarians," 1994.

Law Librarians Society of Washington, DC
- Secretary/Treasurer, 1995–96.

Figure 9.8. Sample Resume—Leigh Whitney-Jenkins

Leigh R. Whitney-Jenkins

931 W. 60th Ave.
Portland, OR 91110
Office: 612-555-2929

OBJECTIVE: **To work as a Marketing and Events Coordinator with Kastle Corporation.**

HIGHLIGHTS OF QUALIFICATIONS

- Broad experience in customer service.
- Knowledge of marketing in the field of librarianship.
- Experience in planning and implementing client programs in library environments.
- Master's degree in Library Science.

WORK EXPERIENCE

Client Representative, Vista Library Services, Portland, OR, 1992–present.
- Managed 3 large accounts including Oregon Alliance of Research Libraries.
- Reviewed all major documentation produced by training team.
- Directed all aspects of VISTA's Annual Users Group Meeting.
- Represented VISTA at national conferences.

Coordinator of Library Automation, Hearst Foundation Library, Los Angeles, CA, 1991–92.

- Managed all aspects of automation including CD-ROMs, personal computers, DEC local area network, and Internet access.
- Planned and implemented new circulation system.
- Supervised 2 full-time employees and hourly assistants.

User Services Librarian, Fielding Enterprises, Inc., Costa Mesa, CA, 1989–91.

- Served as acquisition specialist, with additional concentration in cataloging/authority control, serials, and overlay processing.
- Performed training sessions on a regular basis.
- Assisted clients in troubleshooting any problems.
- Improved service by designing online client profile to track problems.

Reference Librarian, Loyola University Library, Chicago, IL, 1991.

- Provided reference service, with emphasis on business.
- Taught patrons to use a variety of CD-ROM products.
- Reviewed training manuals for reference support staff.

Project Manager, Africana Retrospective Conversion Project, University of Illinois, Chicago, IL, 1990.

- Oversaw retrospective conversion of Africana materials from the Jason R. Tannon Collection (approximately 20,000 volumes).
- Prepared all authority work.
- Supervised 2.5 staff and hourly assistants.

EDUCATION

M.L.I.S./M.S. (Master of Library and Information Science/Management Information Systems), Rosary College, River Forest, IL, 1991.

B.A., Economics, Stanford University, Palo Alto, CA, 1989. Graduated cum laude.

PROFESSIONAL AND OUTSIDE ACTIVITIES

Special Libraries Association
- Chair, Advertising and Marketing Division, 1993–94. Coordinated publication of directory of libraries providing advertising reference.
- Member, Information Futurists Caucus.

Oregon Outdoors and Fishing Association
- President, 1995–96

10 THE COVER LETTER

In this chapter we are going to learn how to tailor a cover letter successfully, a task that some resume writers find especially difficult to complete. To simplify the process, we'll break it down in several steps and use Janet Taylor as an example. As we examine each step, keep these guidelines in mind:

- Keep the cover letter short and to the point.
- Use it as an opportunity to demonstrate your knowledge of the library or organization to which you are applying—show that you have done your homework.
- The employer will be evaluating your writing skills as he or she reads your cover letter.
- Show the employer how your experience relates to the job—focus on how your skills will benefit the employer.
- Specifically address the required qualifications if you are responding to an advertisement.
- The tone of the letter should be upbeat, positive, and enthusiastic.
- The cover letter provides you with an opportunity to reveal your personality.
- Just like the resume, check and recheck for typos, grammar, and neatness.

STEP 1: ADDRESS AND SALUTATION

Place your address, telephone number, and the date at the top right margin. Below that, at the left margin, give the name and address of the person or organization you're contacting. Exercise caution when you don't know the name of the hiring official; this often happens when you are applying for a position listed in a newspaper or professional journal that asks you to respond to "Search Committee" or "Human Resources Department." Never assume the gender of the individual you are addressing. When you are unable to ascertain an appropriate name, a phrase such as "To whom it may concern" or "Dear Search Committee" is the best alternative.

In applying for a specific job opening (shown in Figure 10.1) Janet Taylor uses the following salutation:

Figure 10.1. Job Ad Janet Taylor Decides to Answer
Library Director. Public Library of Youngstown and Mahoning County serves a population of 250,000, with a staff of 75, main library, 4 branches, Dynix system, and a budget of $5.2 million, in a university community. We seek a dynamic leader who puts service first and has proven communication skills, financial expertise, and knowledge of library automation and electronic resources. Must be effective with library board, public officials, library support organizations, and the community. Qualifications: MLS from an ALA-accredited program and 5 yrs.' professional management experience in a public library. Submit letter and resume to: Audrey Johnson, Youngstown Public Library, 305 Wick Avenue, Youngstown, OH 44503

---

27 Chelsea Court
Woodland Springs, AR 72764
May 1, 1996

Audrey Johnson
Youngstown Public Library
305 Wick Avenue
Youngstown, OH 44503

Dear Ms. Johnson:

STEP 2: THE OPENING PARAGRAPH

In the first paragraph, say why you are writing (state the name of the position) and how you heard about it. If you have been referred to the individual by a mutual acquaintance, be sure to indicate their name. You can also use a "hook" sentence to immediately grab the reader's attention. This sentence should describe how your qualifications relate to the specific position. It can also identify a unique ability, skill, or knowledge that would be especially desirable to the employer.

Janet Taylor might use this opening paragraph:

> I am writing in response to your advertisement for the position of Library Director for the Public Library of Youngstown and Mahoning County, which appeared in *American Libraries*, February 1996. As an Assistant Director in a rapidly growing public library system like Youngstown, I offer strong leadership and management experience as well as a solid record of community involvement.

The second sentence provides that attention-grabbing hook—Janet successfully draws a parallel between her library experience and that of the target position.

STEP 3: THE SECOND PARAGRAPH

Before writing this paragraph, carefully review the qualifications in your resume and focus on the two that are most important—in other words, those that best sell you to the employer. Think carefully about how your skills and abilities meet the needs of the library. Again, demonstrate what you know about the library or organization. You might also indicate *why* you are attracted to the position or library or organization—for example, your record of strong community outreach, the innovative use of technology, or the rapidly expanding public library system.

Here's Janet's second paragraph:

> You will note in my resume that I have experience in virtually every area of public library administration. As part of a team that manages over 100 employees and a budget of $4 million, I bring strong skills in strategic and fiscal management.

Remember, keep thinking like the employer—what will be of greatest interest to their library.

STEP 4: THE CLOSING PARAGRAPH

End your letter with a positive statement and indicate what you would like to happen next. For example, request an interview, say that you will be calling, or that you would like to meet at their earliest convenience.

I would like to tell you more about my accomplishments and I would welcome the opportunity to discuss this position with you. Please contact me at my office at 501–555–1415.

Sincerely,

Janet F. Taylor

Your cover letter should have the same typeface as your resume and should be printed on the same type of paper. Now, let's take a look at some other cover letters for resumes in this book.

SAMPLE COVER LETTERS

Remember, the cover letter should be short and showcase your strongest qualifications.

Kenneth Lanahan is applying for a position as life sciences librarian in the science library, Antioch College. In addition to an M.L.S degree, the position requires "academic degree or extensive experience in science; demonstrated knowledge of microcomputers and electronic information resources; and excellent oral and communication skills." Look at Figure 10.2 to see how skillfully Kenneth has used these buzz words to describe why he is best suited for the position.

Madeline Andrus has just graduated from library school and is applying for her first professional librarian position. She is applying for librarian I/bibliographer in social sciences and journalism in an academic library. The position requires working with instructional and research faculty in the college of journalism, developing effective collection strategies, knowledge of a European language, and the ability to communicate effectively. Although Madeline doesn't have a great deal of professional experience, she has demonstrated her major skill areas quite well in the cover letter in Figure 10.3.

Figure 10.2. Kenneth Lanahan's Cover Letter

84 Oak Court #C-1
Knoxville, TN 03210
February 29, 1996

Antioch College
Science Library
Yellow Springs, Ohio 45387

Dear Search Committee:

I have enclosed my resume in response to your recent advertisement in *The Chronicle of Higher Education* for the position of Librarian-Life Sciences in the Antioch Science Library. With more than four years experience as an academic science librarian, I am especially well-suited to working in Antioch's innovative library environment.

In addition to completing an M.L.S., I have a graduate degree in zoology. My career has focused on providing a high level of service to clients: first to 50 corporate scientists and presently to students in a busy science library. In all of these positions, I have used a wide range of science databases and provided expert microcomputer support.

I would welcome the opportunity to discuss my qualifications for this position and I appreciate your consideration of my resume.

Sincerely,

Kenneth Lanahan

Figure 10.3. Madeline Andrus's Cover Letter

311 W. Chestnut Street
Milwaukee, WI 53222
May 3, 1996

Helen Walden
Undergraduate Library
University of California, Los Angeles
Box 2445
Los Angeles, CA 94115

Dear Ms. Walden:

I am responding to your advertisement in *Library Jobline* concerning the Librarian I/Bibliographer in Social Sciences and Journalism in the Undergraduate Library. My strong communication skills and subject expertise in journalism are particularly well-suited to this position.

With a B.A. in journalism and an M.L.I.S. with course work in collection development, I have provided extensive reference service to university students and enjoy the challenge of a busy reference desk. My writing and bibliographic skills have been honed as a technical writer.

I am anxious to learn more about this position and how my broad range of skills can be of service to the Undergraduate Library. I can be reached during the day at 414-555-4313.

Sincerely,

Madeline C. Andrus

11 CONCLUSION: NOW THAT YOUR RESUME IS DONE

It's a wonderful feeling to know that your resume is in great shape. By following the steps in this book, you now have all the elements at hand to customize your resume for virtually any position. And with that top-notch resume comes the promise of an interview! Even though you don't have an interview scheduled yet, this is a good time to start thinking about this stressful process. Under the best of circumstances, interviewing is not an easy task. A recent survey by OfficeTeam of 1,000 executives nationwide revealed some of the strange but true things that have occurred during interviews:

- One candidate arrived at the interview in a suit—with price tags dangling from the sleeve
- An interview was scheduled to be held in Decatur, Illinois— the job applicant showed up in Decatur, Georgia
- During the interview the applicant's cellular phone rang— and she answered it!

Source: Cullen, Scott, "Inhumane Resources." *Office Systems* 13:10 (Oct. 1996), p. 6.

Sound amazing? Trust me, most seasoned interviewers could quickly add to the list. Take some time now to review the following tips so you will be ready when the employer calls. These tips are divided into three categories: interview preparation, interviewing techniques and strategies, and interview followup.

PREPARING FOR THE INTERVIEW

Most job applicants don't think about formal preparation for an interview, but careful planning will greatly reduce your stress level on the day of the interview. Think of yourself as being in training for the Interview Olympics—remember that only one contestant will get that gold medal: the job! So get ready for anywhere from four to five hours of preparation. Here are some steps to follow:

1. Start thinking like the employer, just as you did with the resume, and try to anticipate the types of questions that the potential employer will ask, such as:

   - "What experience have you had with networks and databases?"
   - "How do you keep up with the latest developments in librarianship?"
   - "What has been your greatest supervisory challenge, and how did you deal with it?"
   - "What is your ultimate career goal?"
   - "Have you worked with a team of people?"

2. Once you have completed a set of questions, write down answers. Then, start practicing your responses. Try this with a friend acting as the interviewer and in front of a mirror. You will be amazed at how easily phrases and concepts will come to you during the interview. As with your resume, quantify your answers whenever possible.

3. Think carefully about what you wear and maybe even practice your interview in the clothing you will be wearing for the actual interview—a dress rehearsal! Much ink has been spilled about the right colors and styles to wear during an interview, but suffice it to say that a conservative look is always safest: well-tailored clothing, subdued colors, and restrained jewelry. This is not the time to make a fashion statement, so leave the miniskirts, Donald Duck ties, and three-inch platforms in the closet. Make sure your clothing doesn't distract from your interview. I recall an interview with a candidate who wore a tasteful scarf, but she spent an inordinate amount of time adjusting and readjusting it. Another candidate had exquisite gold bracelets, but continually banged them on the conference table throughout the interview. And every time a particularly dapper gent in a doublebreasted suit shifted in his chair, he struggled in vain to keep his tie from falling out of his jacket.

4. At some point during the interview, the employer will inevitably ask if you have any questions about the position. Make sure you have questions prepared before you arrive for the interview. If you don't express curiosity about the position, this will be a signal to the employer that you are not very interested in the position. Make sure that your questions are focused on the job—not the salary, vacation, benefits, hours, promotional opportunities, size of your office, sick leave, and other trappings.

5. If you haven't been to the library or institution before, go

a day early and find the exact location and room number, if necessary. Nothing will unnerve you quicker than trying to find the location at the last minute.

6. Use contacts to find out as much as you can about who will be interviewing you—what do you perceive they will be looking for?

INTERVIEWING TECHNIQUES AND STRATEGIES

There are some tricks that can make this process go more smoothly for you:

- Arrive at least ten minutes early for the interview. Showing up late is the kiss of death.
- Vary the tone of your voice. Speak slowly and confidently. Don't feel you must rush into a question by talking instantly—pause for a moment if that helps you collect your thoughts. If you feel that you've answered a question inadequately, remember that you can readdress the question in your summary statement at the end of the interview.
- Shake hands firmly. No one likes to grasp a limp hand, better known as the "dead fish." At the other extreme, avoid finger-crushing grips.
- Avoid garlic, onions, or similar foods before the interview.
- Be positive, enthusiastic, alert, and maintain good posture. Display curiosity and active interest in the operations of the library. If you are given a tour, don't be passive; ask questions and draw parallels to your own experience.
- Avoid saying anything negative about yourself—this is not the time for true confession or humility.
- Don't ramble, and stay on the subject. When you have answered the question—STOP! Nothing is more irritating to an employer than to listen to an interviewee go on and on.
- Interviews are extremely stressful, but do your best to smile and not look as though you are being subjected to an inquisition (which in fact may be the case).
- If you are being interviewed by several people, do your best to maintain eye contact with each one. Make sure you address all the participants and don't focus on just one.
- Most interviews end with questions like "Is there anything

else you can tell us about yourself?" or "Anything else you might want to raise?" so by all means don't miss this golden opportunity. Be ready with a closing statement; based on what you have learned during the interview, summarize your strongest points and tell the employer why you want to work for this library.

AFTER THE INTERVIEW

Now that you've survived the inquisition, don't let down completely; by all means, reward yourself by planning something fun after the interview. But *always, always*, send a thank you letter for the interview. This is the chance to personalize your letter and tailor your qualifications based on what you have learned in the interview.

If you don't get the job, call the employer; tell them how much you appreciated the opportunity to interview and that you hope they will consider you for a position in the future or keep you in mind if they hear of other openings in your area of interest. Again, this can be a good opportunity to ask how your resume or interview style might be improved. Remember, the candidate who got the job may not accept at the last minute and you could easily be reconsidered—this happens frequently.

Don't be frustrated if you don't interview well the first time. Interviewing requires lots of practice, and the more you do it the more comfortable you will become.

APPENDIX I: WHAT NOT TO INCLUDE IN THE RESUME

There are a number of items that should *not* appear in your resume. They include:

- *salary requirements.* Compensation requirements are most appropriately discussed at the interview and are rarely mentioned in the resume unless specifically requested in the ad.
- *personal information.* This includes your age, sex, ethnic background, religious or political affiliation, marital status, or children. Also, don't mention weight, height, or other physical characteristics. And don't send a photograph; while this was once considered appropriate, it is rarely done today and I don't recommend it.
- *e-mail address.* You may want to include your Internet address *if* you have a home account, but resist the temptation to use a workplace account. First, there is the ethical issue about personal use of office systems. Second, there is the privacy issue. Network administrators or others frequently have access to all office accounts and you may not care to have your personal e-mail scrutinized in this manner. Remember the maxim that the Internet is a postcard, not a letter.
- *reference information.* Don't include the names of references or their addresses and telephone numbers. This information is best revealed during the interview. While some continue to include the phrase "references available upon request" at the bottom of the resume, I recommend dropping it completely. When references are specifically requested in a job announcement or advertisement, include them at the end of the resume.

A few tips about references. Never give someone's name as a reference without first obtaining permission, and *always* alert them that they may be contacted soon before you give out a name at the interview. Employers can't be expected to have total recall about former employees and will be much more articulate about you if warned in advance that a call may be coming. Nothing irritates an employer more than to receive a blind call for a reference check. Further, it is especially useful if references know something about the type of job for which you have interviewed.

One final note. *Always* make sure that you have the correct phone number for the reference. Prospective employers became especially annoyed if they have to waste precious time finding phone numbers, or worse, call a reference and discover they have changed jobs.

- *information on why you left a position*. Never reveal this on a resume. This information is generally confidential and more appropriately dealt with in the interview.

APPENDIX II: ACTION VERBS THAT GET INTERVIEWS

achieved
accelerated
accessioned
accomplished
acquired
acted
active in
adapted
added
addressed
adjusted
administered
advised
advocated
allocated
analyzed
applied
appointed
appraised
approved
arranged
articulated
assembled
assessed
assigned
assimilated
assisted
assumed
attained
audited
augmented
authorized
balanced
broadened
budgeted
built
cataloged
chaired
changed
clarified
classified

coached
collected
communicated
compared
compiled
completed
composed
conceived
conducted
consolidated
constructed
consulted
contacted
contributed
controlled
converted
corrected
corresponded
counseled
created
critiqued
decreased
defined
delegated
delivered
demonstrated
described
designated
designed
determined
developed
devised
directed
displayed
distributed
documented
doubled
drafted
earned
edited
educated

effected
eliminated
employed
enacted
encouraged
engaged
enlarged
enlisted
established
estimated
evaluated
examined
executed
exercised
exhibited
expanded
expedited
facilitated
finalized
followed up
forecasted
formed
formulated
fostered
founded
functioned
furnished
gathered
generated
guided
halved
handled
headed
helped
identified
illustrated
implemented
improved
improvised
increased
influenced

informed
initiated
innovated
inspected
instituted
instructed
integrated
interpreted
interviewed
introduced
invented
investigated
involved
issued
justified
launched
learned
lectured
led
located
logged
made
maintained
managed
marketed
measured
mediated
modified
molded
monitored
motivated
negotiated
notified
observed
obtained
operated
ordered
organized
oversaw
participated
perceived
performed
persuaded
pinpointed

pioneered
planned
prepared
presented
processed
procured
produced
programmed
promoted
proposed
proved
provided
published
purchased
raised
reallocated
received
recommended
reconciled
recruited
redesigned
reduced
referred
regulated
reinforced
reported
represented
requested
requisitioned
researched
resolved
revamped
reviewed
revised
scheduled
screened
searched
secured
served
serviced
set up
simplified
sold
solved
sparked

spoke
staffed
standardized
started
stimulated
stored
streamlined
strengthened
stressed
stretched
structured
studied
submitted
succeeded
suggested
summarized
superseded
supervised
supplied
supported
surveyed
tailored
taught
terminated
tested
traced
tracked
traded
trained
transferred
transformed
translated
trimmed
tripled
turned
tutored
uncovered
unified
updated
upgraded
used
utilized
verified
won
wrote

GENERAL SUBJECT INDEX

JOB OBJECTIVES AND POSITION TITLE INDEX

WORK HISTORY INDEX
(TO LOCATE A PARTICULAR JOB FOR IDEAS ON USEFUL ONE-LINER DESCRIPTIONS)

ABOUT THE AUTHOR

Robert R. Newlen is a Management Specialist with the Congressional Research Service, Library of Congress, where he has worked for 22 years. He graduated with a B.A. from Bridgewater College, an M.A. from The American University, and an M.S.L.S. from The Catholic University. He is a frequent speaker on resume writing and interviewing. He has served as Director on the Board of the District of Columbia Library Association and is currently a member of the Executive Board of the American Library Association.